Dawn Chan Curtis takes you o̶ through personal highlights of "Miracles." This compelling book is gracious, personal and heartening.

Beverly Jean Day, ND, MBA
Traditional Naturopath

This is a book full of grace from God; a book about how a Christian can know God personally to discern His voice and will. I have known Dawn for many years and have seen how she has navigated a lot of her ups and downs in life with the realization that God is the one in control. Every incident she described in the book was so unbelievably challenging, and miraculously taken care of by God. Praise the LORD for this testimony!

Daisy Fung
Pastor

It was encouraging to read *Miracles...and Beyond* because through it, you can see how God works in other people's lives. Dawn writes with a sincere heart, unafraid to share doubts and struggles. In the end, what matters is that we trust God through it all and she makes this point very clear. Knowing Dawn makes this book even more special to me. You'll want to share this book with others!

Damon Hodges
Elder, Naples Church of Christ

Dawn's book is quite the testimony of experiencing God's miracles today! Her story shares how God intentionally sought her out and desired a deeper relationship with her. As her attention centered around Him, she began to see and hear Him more clearly! God's signs and miracles were the evidence that He is always present and active in her life. Her experiences encourage me to stay alert to how God personally wants to interact with me.

Donna Hodges

Women's leader, Naples Church of Christ

Miracles...and Beyond

FIRSTHAND EXPERIENCES THAT TRANSFORM AND INSPIRE

Dawn Chan Curtis

NEW HARBOR PRESS

RAPID CITY, SD

Curtis/New Harbor Press
1601 Mt. Rushmore Rd., Ste 3288
Rapid City, SD 57701
www.NewHarborPress.com

Ordering Information:
Quantity sales. Special discounts are available on quantity purchases by corporations, associations, and others. For details, contact the "Special Sales Department" at the address above.

Miracles...and Beyond/Dawn Chan Curtis. —1st ed.
ISBN 978-1-63357-354-3
Library of Congress Control Number: 2020920360

To the two most important men in my life:

My precious son Rex Tsun Cheung

and

My husband, pastor, and best friend Steve Frank Curtis

Contents

Preface

The publishing of *Miracles...and Beyond* is taking place during one of history's most challenging times, when the Covid-19 pandemic is wreaking havoc on people's daily living all over the world. My two home countries, Hong Kong and the US, are suffering even further because of widespread social unrest brought about by various political and human rights issues.

National lock-downs, social distancing, deaths, unemployment, bankruptcies, widespread protests, riots, looting, national conflicts, religious and political persecution and so on are happening almost every day during this period. Truths and lies are so mixed up in the media that we don't know which source of information to rely on. It has become difficult especially for people in Hong Kong to express their viewpoints and preferences with confidence or without fear.

I am humbled to see that my book could be launched against this background. I am deeply grateful for all the open doors that allow my voice to be heard at least within the Christian circle. The scale and magnitude of the personal "adventures" I write about in this book can, by no means, be compared with what is happening around the world. But I believe that all kinds of struggles, whether personal or national, are of similar nature when God himself is involved.

The fierce battles we are facing and dealing with every day, be it Covid-19, the fight for freedom and human rights, national conflicts, terminal illnesses, persecution, relationship break ups, office politics, gossips, or even as small as the fight between two kids, are and have always been of spiritual origin and can only be resolved on a spiritual level. Even natural disasters can be traced back to human evil that originated from the time of Adam and Eve.

The Bible says that everything happens because of what happens inside the human heart. And it is often the invisible that is the most influential.

> *Above all else, guard your heart, for everything you do flows from it. (Proverbs 4:23 NIV)*

> *For our struggle is not against flesh and blood, but against the rulers, against the authorities,*

against the powers of this dark world and against the spiritual forces of evil in the heavenly realms. (Ephesians 6:12 NIV)

By the grace of God, I have gone through fierce battles against my own darkness, and was offered a glimpse of God's power and glory when he delivered me, transformed me and showered me with miraculous blessings that I don't deserve. What truly matters in this book is not the stories of miracles, or the presence or absence of miracles, but who is actually behind the scene.

I wish my readers, having read my book, will not casually dismiss any spiritual encounters as mere ghost stories or fairy tales, but will start to see and experience how close we are and how much we can be affected by what is happening in the spiritual realm.

I also hope that you will see God's heart for us, that he is always fighting on our behalf (if we allow him to) even when no miracle is in sight on earth. All battles belong to God:

This is what the Lord says to you: 'Do not be afraid or discouraged because of this vast army. For the battle is not yours, but God's.' (2 Chronicles 20:15b NIV)

The battles are fierce, but our almighty God always wins. The ultimate victory belongs to him.

Part 1: Introduction and Overview

CHAPTER 1

The Decision to Write

Why Wait Until Now?

Before I started writing this book, I asked myself a few critical questions. Why didn't I write to tell the world about the miraculous experiences as soon as they happened? Why did I wait so long? Why is it time to write now?

It has been almost a decade since I literally saw God's warning on an e-mail urging my departure from running a school steeped in New Age practices. And it has been over seven years since I experienced a miraculous five-minute complete healing from a serious flu in Portugal. There have also been numerous signs spanning a period of a few years that eventually led to my second marriage with a pastor in the US in 2015. And then

I heard God's voice and felt a vibration in my left ear in 2018.

Why didn't I write about it? I think the most important reason was that I was afraid of giving people the wrong idea about me—that I am irrational, overimaginative, ungrounded, indulging in wishful thinking, or mentally ill.

Also, I did not want to give believers the impression that I was chasing after miracles in order to experience God. Over the years, I have been extremely cautious in choosing who to tell and what to tell. I dreaded the possibility that I might mislead certain new believers to think that we need to experience miracles to have a close and solid relationship with God. God makes it clear that faith comes by "hearing the message, and the message is heard through the word about Christ" (Rom 10:17 NLT). We don't need to see "miracles" in order to build faith and become strong believers:

> Now faith is confidence in what we hope for and assurance about what we do not see. This is what the ancients were commended for. (Heb. 11:1–2 NIV)

> Then Jesus told him, "Because you have seen me, you have believed; blessed are those who

have not seen and yet have believed." *(John 20:29 NIV)*

Furthermore, God did not give me an urge to write earlier. I was overwhelmed by the miraculous experience each time; and in many instances, I was actually compelled to kneel immediately to thank God for his help or to cry out to God for mercy and further guidance. But I did not feel the urge to write and announce to the world what I had experienced. I did think of writing, and I did ask God for a go-ahead signal, but I did not perceive any answer from him. God's silence seemed to be saying, "Not yet." Deep down inside me, I believed that if God wanted me to do this, he would give me signs and direction.

The Urge to Write

Having said this, it almost goes without saying that I have the urge to write now. Yes, I think this urge was prompted after I literally heard God's voice while I was lying in bed sick and thinking of a plan to leave my new home in the US and go back to Hong Kong to seek medical help in October 2018. This incident will be reported in detail in Chapter 10. This unexpected and overwhelming encounter with God led me to pray fervently, asking God what he wanted me to do; and if writing a book was one of the things, I asked him to please open doors and give me some signals. I vaguely knew that privileges and gifts usually come with more responsibilities and account-ability. Then two things happened that helped me nail down the writing project.

Around the end of 2018, my friend, Dr. Bev Day, a naturopath, invited me to coauthor a book that she thought I had the expertise and experience to write. This was very humbling, and I gladly accepted it as I thought this would be a learning journey for me even if, for some reason, we might not be able to complete the project.

So, we started to have meetings and discussions, and Bev gave me two reference books about how to write a book. During the process of discussion and reading, instead of thinking single-mindedly on how to write that book, the thoughts and vision in my mind were more about planning and writing out the miracles that have been in my heart for many years. I felt the urge to write not about the subject we were working on, but about what God has done for me.

I continued to pray for God's direction. Then one day, a health professional sent in a link that talked about how a woman was miraculously healed of her stage 4 breast cancer during a vivid encounter with Jesus. I was highly curious, so I clicked on her video and discovered that she had written a book too! The book is called *The*

Conversation in Heaven.[1] I bought the book and immediately read it, then felt greatly encouraged by the author's faith and courage to testify to the world about God's power and grace.

During the search online for *The Conversation in Heaven*, I also came across *The Case for Miracles* by Lee Strobel.[2] Strobel had thoroughly researched every aspect of miracles and beautifully contrasted and balanced various experts' viewpoints to conclude that miracles are possible and that God still intervenes to work wonders in people's lives. After gulping down his book in about a week, my hesitation about writing was gone. I started to see God's plan for me in this project. He understood my hesitation and graciously surrounded me with friends, tools, and examples so that I could take my first step forward.

My Hope and Vision for This Book

Taking up the pen to write a book about how God is working in my life is a solemn and sacred event. It is an act to glorify God, and it is more about God than about me and my life, but a brief background about myself

---

1. Holt-Jennings, Abigail. The Conversation in Heaven: Living Life's Ups and Downs Through Heaven's Lens. City of Publication: Publisher, 2018.

2. Strobel, Lee. The Case for Miracles. Grand Rapids: Zondervan, 2018.

might help you navigate through the book with greater understanding.

A Brief Background of Myself

I am Dawn Chan Curtis, a full-blooded Chinese. Curtis is the surname of my husband, an American now pastoring a church in Texas.

I was born in 1964 and raised in a big traditional Chinese family of nine (two parents and seven siblings) in Hong Kong. My parents were unchurched and followed practices of ancestral worship handed down to them by their parents. I was introduced to Christianity by my sister, Sarah, and became a Christian at a summer camp organized by a church when I was twelve years old. I can still remember an evening at the camp, in a hall full of kids around my age, how I was deeply convicted of my pride and selfishness and felt an urge inside to confess my sins and accept Jesus as my Savior. I was moved to tears when we sang a song with lyrics in Chinese that said, "If anyone is in Christ, he is a new creation. The old has gone, the new has come." Throughout my teenage years and early twenties, I was deeply involved in Christian activities.

In 1987, I graduated from the University of Hong Kong with a double major in philosophy and English literature. During my undergraduate years, I worked hard not only in my studies but also in earning money through private tutoring to provide for my independent living. I became the chief editor of an intercollegiate Christian magazine in my final year of study. Most of my after-school and after-work hours were spent brainstorming ideas, researching relevant Christian topics for students, and writing and editing articles. I did not have a lot of fellowship with other Christians though. My faith was more on an intellectual level.

After graduation from the university and, more so, after a few years' work in the public relations field, my whole focus shifted to dating, marriage, and building up my career. I got married to my first husband in 1992 and gave birth to my only son in 2002. I started my own public relations firm a few years after getting married. It gradually expanded from a solo company to a twelve-person-strong agency. We served many big international companies on both corporate communications and consumer retailing levels. I worked day and night. It would not be an exaggeration to say that I was chasing after material wealth, success, recognition, and self-fulfillment to the extent that I was a Christian in name only.

Then came my slide into the darkest valley of my life, when my husband and I separated in 2004. It was mostly my fault. I was eventually divorced by my husband despite my repentance and repeated efforts to reconcile with him through marriage counseling. I was devastated.

For at least six to seven years, I lived under great remorse, regret, and denial. I sold my public relations firm to become a full-time mom in 2007 because I knew I could not afford to miss the important foundation years of my son who was already five years old at the time. I came to realize that relationships were the most important things in life. I was willing to give up my business to minimize the damage I was doing to my family.

After retiring from the public relations field, I became intensely interested in natural healing, especially aromatherapy. I took a two-year diploma course to become a certified aromatherapist in Hong Kong, and thereafter, I pursued three levels of advanced clinical aromatherapy in France. Around that time, the aromatherapy school in Hong Kong I graduated from was running at a loss and planning to close down. My passion, plus my ambition, prompted me to commit to a rescue plan for the school. By the end of 2009, I became the school's major shareholder, tutor, and therapist. Within a couple of years, I turned the business around on all levels. But then I realized this was not God's plan for me. A series of unusual events took place that awakened me to my spiritual crisis and eventually forced me to quit and sell all my shares (see Chapter 6).

I repented. I could see the ambitious Dawn striving to mend the holes and brokenness in her life by holding onto something that seemed to give value and affirmation. When I took up the business of the aromatherapy school, I was repeating the mistakes and patterns of the past. I did not check the inventories of my life and, in particular, my spiritual being, to regain an honest view of my soul. I knew I had to let go and be completely quiet and empty in front of the Lord to seek and find his will for my life.

I started to dig deeper into God's Word and reconnect with fellow Christians. I returned to God with all my heart. I looked daily at the following passage from Isaiah to remind myself to get back on track:

> This is what the Lord says—your Redeemer, the Holy One of Israel:
> "I am the Lord your God,
> who teaches you what is best for you,
> who directs you in the way you should go.
> If only you had paid attention to my commands,
> your peace would have been like a river,

your well-being like the waves of the sea."
(Isaiah 48:17–18 NIV)

Once I stopped striving for myself and let God work on me, I saw his wonders and fingerprints all over my life again. He had never moved; I had. God graciously gave me a second marriage in 2015, plus all the avenues to serve him and his people in both the US and Hong Kong. I have witnessed the work of his hands and tasted his goodness and mercy. I am grateful beyond words. It makes me excited to think about what adventures are still to come as God reveals himself in wondrous ways.

An Invitation to Experience God Together

Now that I have set my mind to write and glorify God, I am no longer bothered by thoughts that people might reject or disagree with this book. After all, it is not about me; it is about *him*. Just as, in the Bible, people could reject and deny God even in the face of miracles, people nowadays can do the same thing and dub miracles as mere coincidences, hallucinations, or wishful thinking. Surely there have been fake miracles and claims that put shame on all Christians. And there are still numerous theological viewpoints that say God no longer works miracles after Christ's death and resurrection.

If you are interested in going deeper into the theology, critiques, and evidence for miracles, I encourage you to read Strobel's *The Case for Miracles*. Here, I invite you to walk with me to see for yourself all the supernatural events and miracles that have dotted and transformed my life, and, hopefully, we can testify together to God's existence and praise him for his goodness, power, and unfailing love. Perhaps you will begin to recognize miracles in your life too!

CHAPTER 2

Clarifying Some Terms and Concepts

Supernatural Events Versus Miracles

Not all supernatural experiences are from God. That's my belief. For clarity's sake, I would like to define "supernatural event" as any event that science cannot explain according to the law of nature, and the cause of its happening or the force behind it doesn't necessarily come from God. I prefer to reserve the word "miracle" for any supernatural event that is a result of prayers and God's intervention, events that refresh and restore the spirit and lead to positive impact and outcome.

I make note of the difference between these two terms because I did experience supernatural events that haunted me when I was younger, and with hindsight and greater understanding of our God, they were obviously not divine interventions for my good.

Not Everything Spiritual Is Good

If you believe in God, you believe in the existence of the spiritual world. The Bible talks about the existence of spiritual beings other than God, and in particular, Satan, the dark force behind the world ever since the fall of human beings.

I am about to tell some of my spiritual encounters or encounters with spiritual beings that were not from God in the second part of this book. When I say they were not from God, I actually have the idea that they were from Satan. I cannot, however, simply refer to them as forces from Satan because I don't have any objective proof of their identities or origin in most cases. All I have are purely personal and subjective experiences, experiences in contrast to those I have with our all-powerful, all-good, and loving God.

Recounting these stories is difficult because they were very unpleasant. It was not that there were monstrous, eerie, or ghastly faces or figures such as those featured in horror movies. No, not at all. It was the supernatural force and power of the unknown, the dark despair it elicited, or the emptiness it entailed that was extremely haunting.

I have no intention to create the goosebumps, nor to spark off a theological debate on the nature and operation of Satan. All I would like to achieve is to enable you to see more clearly the reality of the spiritual realm and become more cautious when you are invited to probe into those areas. You will be surprised by how many different faces and avenues evil spirits can take to influence us and lure us away from God. It is therefore important to be especially careful and discerning.

> *Dear friends, do not believe every spirit, but test the spirits to see whether they are from God, because many false prophets have gone out into the world. (1 John 4:1 NIV)*

> *The coming of the lawless one will be in accordance with how Satan works. He will use all sorts of displays of power through signs and wonders that serve the lie, and all the ways that wickedness deceives those who are perishing. They perish because they refused to love the truth and so be saved. (2 Thess. 2:9–10 NIV)*

As a side note, one interesting observation is that many people are interested in the spiritual realm, yet choose not to believe in God. They believe in and are excited (or scared) by eerie ghost stories, psychic reading, and fortune-telling, but they do not care for a God who created all things and is above all things in the universe. I find this intriguing. If we believe that there is a spiritual world, why not be driven to learn if there is a God who is "far above all rule and authority, power and dominion" (Eph. 1:21a NIV)? Why are some of us scared of ghosts and darkness, yet not actively searching for the almighty God who is the life and the light?

Satan trembles in front of God. It is with this truth in mind that I can talk and discuss about my encounter with darkness without the fear of being engulfed by it.

Part 2: Not All Supernatural Experiences Are from God

CHAPTER 3

A Dangerous Game

I have five older sisters and one younger brother. During my childhood, my father was a seaman and was seldom at home. My mom worked as a maid at other people's homes, and apart from making meals for us, her key focus was to earn more money. So, the seven of us were basically under little supervision. I saw my sisters as my best playmates. Whatever they did, I gladly followed.

When I was still in the primary school, one of my sisters introduced us to a new game called the Ouija Board. We created our own Ouija Board by using a big piece of paper with twenty-six letters and ten numbers (zero through nine) written on it in two circles, respectively. In the center of the paper, a coin was placed. The coin was considered a fairy, a being that was like the genie in the story of Aladdin. All those who participated in the game had to place their pointer fingers on the coin to start the game. Once all participants had decided on a question to ask the "Coin Fairy," they would call upon the fairy, then ask the question together. The coin was supposed to start moving and stop on certain letters to make a word or words, thus giving the answer.

Learning about the game made us all excited. We started to play the game without thinking and without knowing what could be the force behind the coin.

I remember we started with some simple questions to test the Coin Fairy out, questions such as, What kind of food did we eat yesterday? What is the name of my father? and so on. The answers were always correct! We suspected the coin was pushed by some of us who had the gift of spelling, but none of us admitted that.

We then became more daring and asked questions about the future, questions such as, What will happen to us in a few years? When will we get married? What will be the four winning numbers of the upcoming lottery? and so on. The answer to my question of, "How old will I be when I get married?" did not please me though. The Coin Fairy said I would get married at the age of thirty. This was too late for our society at that time. I was, however, not troubled for too long because I knew it would take many years to get this verified. My first marriage came at the age of twenty-seven. Hopefully, this was not due to a subconscious determination to disprove the "prophecy".

One of my sisters got an answer that made her really excited. The Coin Fairy said she would travel overseas to study. This indeed happened a few years later, and my sister connected this to the Ouija Board game. We were all intrigued, I believe; but for some reason, none of us followed up on the whole mystery.

As for the question about the lottery, we could verify the answer in just a few days, and the Coin Fairy got three out of the four numbers right! Although it did not get all four right, we still found it incredible and encouraging as the pool of numbers in the lottery was big. It seemed this had to come from somebody who could partially predict the future but yet was not fully omnipotent.

With this and many other instances, we were convinced that the force was not from any of us. But instead of feeling scared, our curiosity grew, and we became more ambitious with the game.

"Who Are You, Coin Fairy?"

We asked more questions about our future; we even asked who the Coin Fairy was. We knew if we received a reply to this last question about the identity, it would be the most revealing and exhilarating moment of all. And yes, we did receive the answer!

The coin moved to spell out the word "ANCESTOR," a word that none of us understood at that time. So, we went to an English-Chinese dictionary to check out the meaning. "Family members who lived before us," it said. We were both astounded and at ease with this. We, as well as many Chinese people in Hong Kong and mainland China, worshipped our ancestors. Traditionally, the Chinese believe that our souls live forever after we die. Ancestor worship is a religious practice passed down from ancient times to express our filial piety, respect, and gratitude toward our predecessors. My parents set up shrines at home with wooden tablets inscribed with words like, "To all the previous generations of ancestors under the clan of CHAN [our family name]." They burned incense for them every day and offered sacrifices like food and drinks and paper money on important occasions such as the Chinese New Year and Tomb Sweeping Festival. It was believed that ancestors, when well respected and provided for, would protect their descendants and give them prosperity. They were seen as ghosts with some supernatural power and obviously had needs and desires (e.g., for food and wealth) like all of us too. So, the answer given by the Coin Fairy was logical and acceptable for us at that time. It reinforced our belief in and worship of the ancestral spirits. As a little girl, my only question was why our ancestors were suddenly able to write in English.

God was merciful. I vaguely remember we stopped playing the game soon after this, probably because we caught the attention of some adults who thought stepping into the spiritual realm or interfering with ancestral spirits was dangerous or not respectful.

When the Coin Fairy Met the Cross

Now with hindsight as a Christian, I can see how Satan was trying to lure us away from God into his area of control by masquerading as deceased family members and as spiritual beings with kind intentions and supernatural power. I have goosebumps every time I recall the event.

Why am I so sure the force behind the coin was not from our heavenly Father? According to my sister Sarah (the one who brought me to Christ), as she recalled years later, the coin did not move whenever a friend of ours, Mary (a pseudonym), joined in the game. And Mary wore a cross pendant on her chest. Such realization led Sarah to appreciate the power of Jesus, and she became a Christian a few years later.

Numerous passages in the New Testament show that demons or evil spirits are afraid of God. They begged Jesus not to destroy them but let them go:

Just then a man in their synagogue who was possessed by an impure spirit cried out, "What do you want with us, Jesus of Nazareth? Have you come to destroy us? I know who you are— the Holy One of God!"

"Be quiet!" said Jesus sternly. "Come out of him!" The impure spirit shook the man violently and came out of him with a shriek. (Mark 1:23-26 NIV)

The same happened when Mary joined in our Ouija Board game. I am not saying an ornament in the shape of a cross can by itself dispel demons or evil spirits. This would be idolatry. But it could be that Mary was a devoted Christian and that God's Spirit filled her and protected her that day. Somehow, God's presence stopped the work of the Coin Fairy just as Satan was in fear and could not function in the presence of God in Mark 1. Our God is bigger than anything in heaven and earth.

...that at the name of Jesus every knee should bow, in heaven and on earth and under the earth. (Phil. 2:10 NIV)

CHAPTER 4

When "Prophetic" Dreams and Experiences Haunt and Disturb

The years between 1998 and 2001 were an eventful and traumatic period for my family of origin in Hong Kong. I had two nightmares that preceded some of these events, and they were almost "prophetic." I don't mean they were prophecies from God. The dreams haunted and disturbed me for quite some time instead of being helpful and directional. I doubt if God will haunt and disturb us for no special reason.

I had experiences of a prophetic nature even when I was a child. Some call it a sixth-sense experience. It was scary instead of inspirational and instilled a feeling of helplessness instead of offering encouragement. It is by looking at characteristics such as these that I discerned if a supernatural experience was from God.

Let me briefly tell you my sixth-sense experience before detailing the nightmares.

I was very young, perhaps seven to nine years old, still a primary school student at a local Chinese school near my home. The school was located on a hill, and there was a very steep, main road that led up to it. One late afternoon after school, while walking down the road, I suddenly had the thought that something unfortunate had happened at home. I felt the urgency and started to run downhill as fast as possible. I still remember the speed of my running, along with the acceleration of my beating heart, and the wind that brushed against my face. When I reached home, I saw that my second sister Rene (a pseudonym), had a deep red wound on her arm, with blood gushing out from the torn tissue. My mother told me she had just been electrocuted by a socket on the wall. There was a lot of movement around me, but surprisingly I don't have any memory of what happened next. The end of this whole experience was frozen with the scene of the wound. I cannot even recall if I told anybody about my panicky run. This was a pure sixth-sense experience.

Stormy Sea

In one of the dreams that I had in 1997, I saw my mom and my second sister Rene riding in a boat in a huge storm. The sky was dark, the wind howled, and waves of water churned and turned the boat over. My mom and sister were hurled into the water. I was not able to help them. For me, it was like watching a movie. Mom was hanging onto a plank of wood floating on the water. My sister was struggling as well, but instead of trying to save herself, she was holding a sharp knife trying to kill herself. Then the scene went forward in time. (It might not have been that abrupt in my dream, but it is in my memory.) Mom put my sister on a wooden bench, and she took care of Rene while complaining about the accident.

What really happened to my mom and Rene? Here's the background and story that took place between 1997 and 1998.

My parents had been distanced from each other throughout their marriage. I attribute this to my father's occupation as a seaman. My father needed to go overseas for his job, and so his time with Mom was less than six months a year. After his retirement in the early eighties, he returned home for good but felt like a stranger to us and his friends. He told us explicitly that he envied

Mom a lot because he felt that we, his children, had less affection for him than for Mom. So, he went back to his hometown in Zhongshan (a county in the southern part of China) to reestablish his life and his career. He opened a small bakery store in San Xiang, a town near his birthplace, and built a house there for the sake of convenience. Being a handsome entrepreneur with a lot of different talents, my father attracted a few women in that area and had a publicly known affair with one of his staff members. The woman got pregnant when my father was almost seventy years old. Mom knew about this affair for several years, but since she did not want to live in or go frequently to San Xiang to keep my dad company, she accepted it.

Mom was devastated when she found out that the mistress was pregnant. She was living with me at that time. The hour that she learned about this, I was on my way home from work. Before opening the door to enter my apartment, I had the feeling that something was wrong. I slowly opened the door and peeped in and saw Mom was sitting on the sofa. I did not see her face, but I cried out to her, "What's happened, Mom?" She did not answer me. I approached her and saw tears welling from her eyes. She told me Dad just informed her of the pregnancy of the woman with whom he had an affair. I still could not understand how Mom had lived with the fact that Dad had been unfaithful to her for so long. It seemed to me that Mom had already overcome the betrayal and the loss of love, but now that the woman became pregnant, the pent-up emotions burst through.

"If the woman's child is a boy, I will jump down from the building," Mom cried out with heartbreaking sobs. My apartment was on the nineteenth floor.

For the traditional Chinese, having a male descendant is of paramount importance and honor to the family. A woman's status is often raised when she gives birth to a son. Mom had tried six times before she finally had a son, my younger brother. It would be unbearable for her to see another woman claiming the same status, let alone sharing her husband.

I forgot totally my reaction toward Mom at that time. I loved my mom so much that I deeply felt her hurts. As in my dream, I saw that she was "drowning," but I could do nothing.

Around that time, also between 1997 and 1998, my second sister Rene moved to live with my father to help him with his bakery business. Rene had suffered failures in a few business ventures in Hong Kong and had accumulated a large amount of debt. She called me (and other members of the family too, I guess) from time to time for money, and she would use all possible means, including suicide threats, to get what she wanted. We all agreed that the best way to "save" her (and probably minimize trouble for us) was to send her away from Hong Kong. And the most convenient option for her was to work for Dad at the bakery shop.

While Rene was living and working in San Xiang, she made friends with people who gambled, and she ran into deeper debt. My father received threats from the gang she owed money to and was greatly troubled. In early 1998, just a few months after his seventy-year-old birthday celebration, my father died from a heart attack in a short span of fifteen to twenty minutes. His mistress gave birth to a girl slightly before he passed away.

While we were still grieving the loss of our father, Rene suffered a serious brain injury in a traffic accident at the end of that same year. We were told that Rene gambled until after midnight and was then given a ride on the back of a motorcycle. The motorcyclist went too fast, and Rene was flung off the vehicle and landed on the side of a rocky road. Her head was seriously injured. Blood ran out from her ears. She was sent to the intensive care unit of a local hospital.

A few of us arrived at the hospital the next day. The ICU was a shabby room with the most backward life-saving equipment that I had ever seen. A dead cockroach was lying in a corner near to the entrance. Rene was stretched out on a bed in a coma. Her hair was all shaved off, and her head was fully bandaged. After looking at the facilities and the hygienic conditions of the hospital, we decided to bring her back to Hong Kong. We would do all we could to save her life despite the very slim hope. After a long surgery and intensive care in a Hong Kong public hospital, Rene eventually escaped death. The doctor in charge said that because of the serious brain damage, Rene might never regain consciousness even if there was no threat of death. We prayed for her day and night. Rene eventually woke up from a coma after a few weeks. However, she lost part of her memory and cognitive function and regressed to a mental age of twelve. She then stayed in a rehabilitation center for almost half a year. After that, Mom, having suffered a series of heartbreaking events herself, rented an apartment to live with and take care of Rene.

Mom and Rene are like friends and foes at the same time. From her youth, Rene had been labeled a problem child in the family. Mom always scolded Rene despite her deep love for her. During the time when Rene was in a coma, Mom sat beside her bed in the hospital all the time. She complained about the accident and dreaded the suffering my sister had caused herself and the family, but she never stopped taking care of her.

My mom is ninety-one years old now. For over twenty years, Mom has walked alongside Rene. Often when I see them together, I am reminded of the scene in my dream where Mom put Rene on a wooden bench, giving her care and support while complaining about the accident.

Change of Appearance

In my second dream that I had a few months before 2001, I saw my brother Alfred (a pseudonym) as a small kid. I carried him onto a bed in a hospital telling him that he didn't have to be afraid because we would take good care of him. In another scene in the same dream, Alfred returned home from the hospital as an adult. As he came through the door, he didn't look the same. His face was not one that I could fully recognize. His appearance had changed.

What happened in reality, in early 2001, was that Alfred's health suddenly went downhill, and he suffered a lot of pain and inflammation in his neck. He had consulted numerous western doctors and had tried various alternative treatments to relieve the pain but to no avail. Then it came to a point that he started losing his balance and could not walk well. He lost hearing in his left ear; his speech was no longer coherent; and he would lose his vision suddenly for eight to ten seconds. After a lot of medical examinations, he was finally diagnosed with a brain tumor that grew close to the brain stem. He also suffered from spondylosis that limited the degree of his neck movement. It was certainly a very critical situation. Surgery was required immediately to remove the tumor. Despite the success of the surgery, it unfortunately caused damage to his trigeminal nerve. This resulted in permanent paralysis of the left side of his face. My brother had been a very handsome guy. This change in appearance was a big blow to him. Besides, his spondylosis grew worse, and his neck and spine became stiff and inflexible. His hurt and pain on both physical and emotional levels were beyond what we could imagine. My heart shuddered and sank whenever I thought of the dream I had about him.

Coming Out from the Shadow of the Dreams

Just as I did not share with others my sixth-sense experience, I have not revealed any of the above dreams to my family. It was years later that I started to think about the meaning and nature of my experiences. Were they prophecies or mere coincidences with realities? And if they were prophecies, what were the purposes behind them? They did not achieve anything for me or my family except for creating in me a sense of horror and helplessness.

It does not seem to me that God would haunt or scare for no special reason. In the Bible, God did reveal terrifying images of the future to some people to warn and prompt them into actions for good. But he never haunted them in a mysterious manner to instill discouragement and despair. For a period, I was tempted to read books about dream interpretations in order to find hints and answers to my longtime puzzle. Some of the literature I studied included concepts that were in conflict with Christianity. Some even talked about past lives and images of ancient religious rituals. I then realized how vulnerable I could be when I tried to find answers apart from God. I became concerned that the dreams could lead me into darkness. It reminded me of the story of Saul in 1 Samuel 28 when he consulted a medium for advice. Anyway, my personal, subjective experience told me that my dreams were more of an experience of darkness than light.

God is light; in him there is no darkness at all.
(1 John 1:5 NIV)

They were surely not from God.

A Christian doctor friend advised me to pray to God to remove this unnecessary and undesirable "spiritual" connection. It might have been a connection established when I was young or when my family worshipped or paid respect to idols and spirits unknown. Whatever the reasons, it was a dangerous place where God didn't want us to dwell.

Nevertheless, God can turn a misfortune into a blessing when we seek him and turn to him. We have never ceased praying for Rene ever since her accident. Mom witnessed the whole process. She became a Christian shortly after Rene woke up from her coma. Although Mom cannot read or write, she has seldom skipped church or missed a sermon on Sundays throughout the past twenty years. Some of her church members told us that Mom was always the first one to arrive at church and pray quietly by herself before the service. She is at peace with what has happened in her marriage and with the challenging situation of Rene and Alfred. She says she is grateful and always gives thanks to the Lord.

With Mom's love and perseverance, Rene is, in general, healthy and well. Her memory and speech are limited, but she can perform most of her daily routine and chores. For over twenty years, she has been taken care of by the same Christian shelter that offers her both jobs and a social life. She can travel within the city by herself. She enjoys singing and painting. She has forgotten most of her past and has become a new person. Rene's story is a miracle itself, and it warrants another book.

As for Alfred, despite a period of depression after the surgery, his belief in the existence of God has empowered him to come to terms with his physical challenges. He has shown tremendous strength and perseverance through numerous surgeries and health crises in the past two decades. He is still in a lot of pain, but he has never given up. He told me he had made it his mission that Mom would be well-supported and taken care of in the last mile of her life journey. He does grocery shopping and cooks for Mom frequently. He cleans, repairs, and fixes things around her house. This is noble. He has all my respect.

Witnessing all these subsequent developments of Mom, Rene, and Alfred enabled me to come out from the shadow of what haunted me and look squarely at the curse. God is light. In him there is no darkness.

> *The light shines in the darkness, and the darkness has not overcome it. (John 1:5 NIV)*

> *You, dear children, are from God and have overcome them [false prophets] because the one who is in you is greater than the one who is in the world. (1 John 4:4 NIV)*

There are things in the spiritual world that we don't understand and don't have to understand. God has provided all that we need to live and thrive.

The Lord our God has secrets known to no one.
We are not accountable for them, but we and
our children are accountable forever for all that
he has revealed to us, so that we may obey all
the terms of these instructions. (Deut. 29:29
NLT)

God knows what is best for us. Trust him when he asks us not to dwell in or reach out for things that would only do us harm or are not constructive in any way.

CHAPTER 5

Angel Channeling Versus Direct Access to God

I owned and operated an aromatherapy school and clinic from late 2009 to mid-2012. Every day during this period, I was surrounded by therapists and students from all walks of life, and many were engaged in other healing modalities such as craniosacral therapy, foot massage, acupuncture, and so on. Don't misunderstand me, these alternative therapies are well-recognized, and many are actually evidence-based and scientifically sound. But when it comes to therapies that are connected to some unknown source of power, such as crystal therapy, pendulum healing, astrology, tarot card reading, and so on, I have great hesitation.

As a shareholder of the school, I thought that as long as I eliminated from my curriculum all those therapies empowered by an unknown energy, and focused instead on the medicinal properties and clinical use of essential oils, the school and the students would be safe. But Satan is a great imitator. People in the healing industry nowadays always talk about love and care, positive thinking, and self-reflection. And with such positive rationale, a member on the board started to include angel channeling (i.e., communication with the so-called "angels" to gain love and light) in our monthly sharing session.

Brenda (a pseudonym), the lady who did angel channeling, was one of our students. One evening in late 2011, Brenda was invited to conduct our monthly sharing session. She brought to the class a bunch of ribbons of different colors and asked each of us to pick one. Then she went to each individual to reveal what situation and emotional condition that person was in based on the ribbon chosen. All participants were thrilled, if not chilled, because Brenda revealed their life situations exactly as experienced and offered many loving comments.

Throughout the sharing session, I was deeply disturbed. I prayed to God to protect the participants and myself and asked God if the source of her energy was from him. I also asked God to take away my fear and to give me the opportunity and courage to glorify him instead of being lured away by the "magic." When it was my turn, Brenda said, "Dawn, I see bright lights around you, and you are very spiritual."

Immediately, I knew it was a chance to speak up, and so I said gently and firmly, "This is probably because I study the Bible a lot these days, and I hope to be connected to God more." My heart was beating very fast while I spoke, and I quietly prayed to God for help and for an ability to differentiate Brenda's "wisdom" and "energy."

God was extremely gracious. He answered my prayer almost immediately as Brenda responded that the Bible was outdated and that there were a lot of other self-help books in the market that she could recommend for my reading. I was both shocked and encouraged when I heard this because I could feel that God was telling me right away that her power was not from him.

> For such people are false apostles, deceitful workers, masquerading as apostles of Christ. And no wonder, for Satan himself masquerades as an angel of light. It is not surprising, then, if his servants also masquerade as servants of righteousness. (2 Cor. 11:13–15 NIV)

The Bible is the word of God.

"Heaven and earth will pass away, but my [God's] words will never pass away" (Matt. 24:35 NIV).

The Bible will never be outdated. God is our sovereign God in the past, present, and future. Whoever encourages others to doubt or depart from the words of God is against God.

Besides, the whole Bible centers on Jesus, and whoever denies the Bible denies Jesus, and vice versa:

> *This is how you can recognize the Spirit of God: Every spirit that acknowledges that Jesus Christ has come in the flesh is from God, but every spirit that does not acknowledge Jesus is not from God.* (1 John 4:2–3 NIV)

A few days after the session, I took courage to text Brenda to tell her she could go directly to God to ask for his help and guidance instead of going through the so-called "angel." God is the one in charge, and everything is under his feet (1 Cor. 15:27). Jesus already died and resurrected to redeem us from our sins so that by faith in him we will be made clean, clothed with righteousness, and reconciled with God. No middleman is required to pray to God or talk with him. We can go directly to our Father's throne as his beloved children.

Besides, angels are mere entities created by God to serve us:

And God never said to any of the angels,

"Sit in the place of honor at my right hand until I humble your enemies, making them a footstool under your feet."

Therefore, angels are only servants—spirits sent to care for people who will inherit salvation. (Heb. 1:13–14 NLT)

And any spirit that does not acknowledge Jesus as Lord is not from God. I thank God that I have had a chance to experience these truths myself.

After this incident, I became more determined to let go of the school. I thought that if I was not able to influence the management, I should not be there to help and indirectly encourage the spread of false teachings. Numerous miracles took place in the subsequent months, which I will detail in the next part of the book. But before I end here, I would like to share one more episode that reassured me of God's revelation about Brenda's "power" and his desire for me to share with others the fierce spiritual battle we Christians were facing.

That year was the first year I attended Bible Study Fellowship (BSF; a worldwide Christian organization that encourages the in-depth study of the Bible). The last day of BSF was always a share day, and it was around the corner. So, I planned to share the above incident. The night before sharing, I felt a little bit uncertain and panicky because I believed it would be a spiritual battle against the dark forces. I prayed to God and asked if he wanted me to stand up to witness for him, and if yes, if he would reassure me once more.

I had been using a publication called *Our Daily Bread* for personal devotion for over a decade. After my prayers that night, I read the passage for May 23, 2012, in *Our Daily Bread*.[3] Titled "Taking Risk," the devotional had a punchy remark that says: "The rewards of witnessing are well worth the risks" (Dennis Fisher).

The Bible passage for the day was about Paul and Barnabas risking their lives to preach the gospel. And in the Reflection and Pray section at the bottom of the page, a prayer ran as follows: "Will you be bold in your witness by giving lost sinners God's words? Jesus will honor your service, and sinners will surely be stirred" (Bosch).

God assured me through the passage that he would provide his Spirit to empower me. With this clear instruction, how could I not witness for God? I took his

---

3 . Our Daily Bread. Grand Rapids: Our Daily Bread Ministries, 2012.

words and promises that night and slept extraordinarily well. As planned, I shared the story of angel channeling at BSF on the morning of May 24, 2012. To give everybody a chance to share, BSF limited each speech to five minutes. I was able to speak every word I had written down just within that time. I felt I had testified to the power of the Lord without any reservation and hesitation. I was overwhelmed by a joy that surpassed my understanding when I finished sharing.

Part 3: Heavenly Miracles

CHAPTER 6

Severe Warning from God in an E-mail

I experienced God's intervention in my life numerous times. In one instance, I felt that he was probably so frustrated with my foolish decisions and inactions that he had to give me obvious warnings, actually black-and-white warnings, to make me change my course.

This happened when I considered selling all my shares in the aromatherapy school and resigning from my roles there as teacher and therapist in 2011. There were many reasons behind my wish to leave the school. An obvious one was the clash of management style with my ex-business partner Angelina (a pseudonym). Our communication had become minimal after a few episodes of misunderstanding, and this made our conflict in management style all the more difficult to overcome.

The other reason was that I found myself deviating from my original goals of becoming a practitioner and educator in the field. As a major shareholder, I was so preoccupied with marketing, enrollment, and administration that I had little time left for professional practice and development. *This is not OK*, I told myself. *I sold my public relations firm previously to give myself more free time to do what I want, and now I am tying myself up again for sales and marketing.*

But as mentioned in the previous chapter, losing control over the school's spiritual direction was what disturbed me most and eventually made me quit the school.

I have to admit that I did not do enough research nor due diligence before I took over the school in 2009. I had little knowledge of Angelina before forging a joint venture with her. I rushed into the business probably because I felt lost in my own life and wanted to hold onto something. The separation from my ex-husband in 2004 had turned my life upside down. I was consumed by bitterness, remorse, and confusion about my life. I sold my public relations firm in 2007 to spend more time with my son, as well as to rethink and reconstruct myself. But I did not ask the Lord what he wanted me to do. I just grabbed whatever came my way.

After selling my public relations firm, which I had run for over twelve years, I studied in Hong Kong to become a certified aromatherapist with the International Federation of Professional Aromatherapists (UK) and the National Association of Holistic Aromatherapists (US). I initially thought it would just be a highly beneficial interest or pastime. But then I became fascinated with the profession and went on to study three more levels of clinical aromatherapy in southern France. By 2009, the aromatherapy school from where I graduated in Hong Kong was closed down. I felt very sorry for it, and I thought that with my entrepreneurial experience coupled with my passion for aromatherapy, I would be able to revive the business and offer more people proper and professional training in the field.

I did revive the business, but I did not bring life to myself and others.

As an aromatherapist and an educator, I got in touch with people from different avenues of the "healing" industry, and a great proportion originated from New Age beliefs and practices. Many teachers and therapists brought into the school healing modalities and philosophies that did not fall into the main streams of alternative healing. I did study some of them, and I have to say not all of them are unfounded. Some are, indeed, great holistic healing methods that touch on the emotional and spiritual levels or employ energy (electromagnetic waves) emitted by us and others for both physiological and emotional healing.

But how about those that advocate universal energy force and wisdom from spiritual beings such as angel channeling? Or those that are related to astrological calculation and prediction? I thought that as long as I did not go into such unknown spiritual realms and the school did not include those ideas in its formal curriculum, the school and I would be fine.

But I was wrong. As a major shareholder, I had all the right to say no and redirect the school back to the right path. But I was too weak and too careless. I feared men more than God. As a Christian and an educator, if I allowed idols and philosophies that contradict Christianity to flow around the school during extracurricular hours, I was actually directing people to spiritual death, and this would definitely displease the Lord.

God was again merciful and forgiving. He made everything work together to warn me and drag me out of the school.

Encouragement to Depart

By summer 2011, my heavy workload plus the clash with Angelina had grown to such an extent that I felt greatly discouraged. I looked for ways to improve the situation, but I failed. The ideas of selling my shares started to sprout. There were many different options to consider. The easiest exit was to find another investor to take up all my shares. But what if no investor was interested? Closing the school would be extremely difficult. Just think of all the existing courses that would need to be completed while the school could no longer bring in new students and income, plus all the refunds we would need to offer to those students who chose not to stay.

One night, I prayed fervently to God to ask for his will and direction for my career. It was the night of August 10, 2011. After I prayed, I read the devotional from *Our Daily Bread* [4] for that day. The passage was Exodus 18:13–27. And the highlighted verse in that Bible passage was, "You will surely wear yourselves out" (Exodus 18:18a NLT). The writer of that day's devotional gave the following advice: "Why not prayerfully discern if there may be tasks you can delegate to others, or even discontinue— so that you don't wear yourself out" (Dennis Fisher). The prayer in the Reflect and Pray section of the devotional voiced out exactly what my heart meant to say:

> Father, we need help with our priorities.
> Teach us to understand what is most important and needs to be accomplished,

---

4 . Our Daily Bread. Grand Rapids: Our Daily Bread Ministries, 2011.

and to let go of what we can so that we are
at our best for you. Amen.

There was even a pithy reminder there to give me
a push: "If we don't come apart and rest awhile, we may
just plain come apart!" (Havner)

I was stunned! I prayed and wrote in my diary:

God, it is so plain and clear to me. Please
help me deal with the departure. I lift to
you all the challenges and complications
of discontinuing my business. Please walk
me through all these difficult circumstances. You are my Lord and my God.

Final Warning

From August to early December of 2011, I did all I
could to find an investor. I talked with many potential
buyers and got one who showed interest, but toward the
end of the year, she backed out. Angelina said she was
not going to buy my shares. So, all my efforts failed. I
did not know what to do when it was almost time to re-
new our office contract. I had to depart. God had shown
me this direction clearly. But I also did not want to just
depart without a dollar recovered. That would mean a
total loss for me. So, I made a transition plan to move

the school to a smaller office with a relatively short contract in the hope of reducing expenses as well as making
preparation for closure. I tried to arrange it in a way that
when all the courses finished, the new office lease would
lapse, and we would be able to close the school.
Just one or two weeks before we needed to move,
Angelina said she would make an effort to find a buyer.
One Sunday night in early December of 2011, I received
her e-mail asking me to meet a potential buyer the next
day. I gladly replied to her and confirmed the meeting
through my iPhone, then went to bed. The next morning, I opened my e-mail account on the computer and
found that under my reply e-mail, a line in Angelina's
message was broken up by a note that said "Romans
1:32." Extremely puzzled, I checked my sent box on my
iPhone, and the same thing happened. Feeling shocked,
I opened the Bible to see what the verse was about:

> *Although they know God's righteous decree*
> *that those who do such things deserve death,*
> *they not only continue to do these very things*
> *but also approve of those who practice them.*
> *(Rom. 1:32 NIV)*

I was alarmed and wondered who sent this Bible verse to me. Was it Angelina who sent this, or was
it a spiritual warning from God? I did not realize the

implication of the Bible verse for me at that time. All I focused on were the two words, "deserve death." I was frightened, confused, and confounded.

I went to a few information technology experts and asked them to help solve the mystery. I asked them if it was possible that some messages could be hidden in an e-mail, then appear only when the receiver of the e-mail pressed the reply button and sent a message back to the sender. They said no. They checked my iPhone and my computer to see if there had been any virus or bug and tried to see if I had done any copy and paste by accident. Nothing was found. I did not read the book of Romans on my iPhone or computer before the incident. I did not push any other buttons apart from making a one-line reply to Angelina that night. I was too tired to do any copy and paste. I thought it was not an accident. It was either from Angelina or it was a supernatural interference from God.

Notwithstanding the puzzle, I went to meet with the buyer. One or two days after that, Angelina said the buyer was willing to acquire the school but at no cost— that is, she was not going to pay me a single dollar for the majority shares. I was asked to leave all the responsibilities behind once the contract was signed.

To me, the offer was unreasonable. The school had a healthy financial record ever since I had taken up the business. It was starting to yield some profits. I thought I had invested a lot of money, effort, and time to turn the business around, so why should I suffer a great loss? I could not make up my mind. I struggled terribly with all kinds of thoughts. Time was running out; the office lease renewal was around the corner. Should I continue the business as it is? Should I go ahead to move and prepare for closure, or should I just quit like nothing has happened in the previous two years?

Just as I was overwhelmed by the Bible verse and all the above thoughts, my good friend Janet (a pseudonym) called. Janet is a psychotherapist and runs a counseling center. We have known each other for over twenty-five years and have kept in touch. It had been more than half a year since Janet had called. On that day, when I was traumatized by all the fears and possibilities, she called. We met for lunch the same day, as she sensed the urgency of my situation. After hearing all that I had gone through in the previous two years, she advised me to find a chance to exit the business as soon as possible. Although Janet did not comment on the appearance of the Bible verse in my e-mail, she probably saw the danger of my further involvement with the school and urged me to leave at all costs. She stressed a few times that I should pray for the next emergency exit that came my way. Well, there had been an exit offered to me by the potential buyer. I refused to accept it. I felt humiliated to sell all my shares for nothing. I was still not able to see the warning behind the Bible verse of Romans 1:32.

That very same day, I had an appointment with my Christian counselor Teresa (a pseudonym). Teresa had known me for a few years and had seen my hurts and wrestling, as well as my growth and recovery ever since the divorce. With all the churning inside my heart, I met her and told her everything that had happened. Teresa gave me the same advice. "Leave at all cost," Teresa said. "Our emotional health is much more precious than the investment."

We prayed together before the session ended. After the prayer, I felt very firm and determined with the idea of selling the business at zero dollars. There was still great pain inside my heart, still a lot of lament for the huge loss of investment, but I knew by then that I needed to obey God and let go. I was ready to give Angelina a call to strike the deal when I got home.

While I was still on my way home, digesting all the messages and advice from Janet and Teresa, Angelina called. She told me the buyer would pay half of what I asked for to take up all the shares. Wow! I could not believe how the situation could change in such a dramatic way when I surrendered and let go. I said yes to her without any hesitation. I was beyond words for the mercy and grace I experienced that afternoon. God listened to our prayers, and he did not leave me empty-handed when I trusted and obeyed.

I suddenly realized that everything that happened in that week, especially the Bible verse, was to make sure that I would take whatever exit available to leave the school. I saw the way God worked. I saw how God cared and loved me to the extent of intervening "physically" into my life, to give me a black-and-white warning about the consequence of death for those who "not only continue to do these very things [allowing idols, angel channeling, and so on in the school], but also approve of those who practice them" (Rom. 1:32). And when I still did not get the message and did not sense the urgency of the situation, he surrounded me with all the people whom I trusted to repeat his urge again and again. If it was not for the Bible verse of Romans 1:32, and if not for all that happened within that week, I doubt if I would have made up my mind to accept the offer so quickly.

God arrested me from being a stumbling block to others. Jesus had made it clear that we should be extremely careful not to lead others to sin:

> Jesus said to his disciples: "Things that cause people to stumble are bound to come, but woe to anyone through whom they come. It would be

better for them to be thrown into the sea with a millstone tied around their neck than to cause one of these little ones to stumble. So watch yourselves." (Luke 17:1–3 NIV)

I wrote in my diary on December 9, 2011, to recount the whole process of departure from the aromatherapy school. Here is what I wrote in the last two paragraphs:

Oh my God, my Lord, I cannot praise you and thank you enough. You are so real and wonderful. You are the one in control. You hear my prayers and put me back on the right path. This past week, I saw how you have intervened and guided me. I have experienced you for myself. And from now on, how should I live for you, God? "Ask and you shall receive." That's what you said to me tonight through your scripture:

That night the Lord appeared to Solomon in a dream, and God said, "What do you want? Ask, and I will give it to you!" (1 Kings 3:5 NLT)

I want a good family, somebody who can walk with me for the rest of my life and to

serve you at my best. God, please show me
in what way you would like to use me.

I did not know at that time what God had planned
for me. But now looking back, he has actually answered
all of my prayers about having a life partner to walk along
with and the opportunity to serve him at my best. This is
another story that I will expound on in Chapter 8.

CHAPTER 7

Immediate and Complete Healing from Sickness

I n February of 2013, during the Chinese New Year holidays, I went to Portugal and Spain for leisure traveling with my son. Ever since my separation from my ex-husband in 2004, holidays and festival celebrations had never been easy, especially that of Chinese New Year when the emphasis on family reunion is super strong. The Chinese still see divorce as a family shame and taboo, and during festive seasons like Chinese New Year, the thought of having a broken marriage can be unbearable. My family never asked me anything about my situation in order not to embarrass me. But the quieter they were, the more hurt I felt. So, I usually went out of town with my son to avoid the disgrace and loneliness of being a single mother.

That year, my son Rex was ten years old. He loved soccer, and Real Madrid was one of his favorite teams. To be safe and to free myself from all kinds of planning, we joined a travel group and set off on February 2 for a ten-day trip to Portugal and Spain.

On the plane, my throat started to feel dry and scratchy. I do not remember exactly what other symptoms I had, but I remember saying to myself, *What a bummer. How can I be sick right from the beginning, when I need to take care of Rex in a foreign land for ten days?*

A Divine Prelude

After a sixteen-hour flight, it was early morning when we arrived in Lisbon, Portugal. According to the itinerary, we were to tour around before settling down in the hotel. That's one of the characteristics of joining a tour group. Every minute was precious, and daytime was maximized by cramming in as much sightseeing as possible.

I remember the last stop of that first day was walking around a famous shopping mall in Lisbon. Holding Rex's hands, I dragged my body through the mall, feeling aches in my lower back. I knew the flu had set in and was escalating. As an aromatherapist, I always carried tiny bottles of essential oils with me for first aid purposes. So, I asked a tour group member to look after my son for a while so that I could go into the bathroom to rub oils on my lower back and have some relief.

After that, though reluctant, I continued to stroll with Rex to browse through store after store. When we came to an eatery, I decided to sit down for a rest and have some food. Right at that moment, I found Rex did not have his jacket with him. His favorite Real Madrid jacket, the one I bought him not long ago, was gone. He must have dropped it somewhere. I knew the chance of finding it was slim. According to the news and information from the leader of the tour group, theft and robbery were rampant in Spain and Portugal. The economies of both countries had suffered great blows just a year or two before our trip. Their currencies had crashed to a very low level while national debts soared sky-high. More than once, we saw policemen arresting thieves on the streets during our tour. So, the hope of finding a lost item was very dim in a high-traffic shopping mall.

I still remember the disappointment and frustration on Rex's face. I quietly cried out to the Lord for help. Then, with the idea of setting a good example for my son, I suggested we pray together at the table. My son said it was OK. So, I prayed out loud for God's peace, comfort, and guidance at this time of loss, physical pain, and challenge. Then we headed back to join the group for departure.

While waiting for other tour members, I told the leader what had happened and asked if there was a lost and found in the mall. The leader was very sympathetic. He pointed us to the service center, which was about a five-minute walk from our place of assembling. I did not hesitate to go to the center. I had a feeling inside me that something unusual might happen. A lady greeted us at the service counter, and we explained what we were looking for.

The lady, with a totally blank expression, asked, "What is the color of your jacket?"

"Bright orange and blue," I said. She bent over to a shelf under the counter and pulled out a jacket.

"Is it this one?"

Wow! What a huge, pleasant surprise! Rex's Real Madrid jacket, with bright orange stripes, was right in front of us! Can you imagine the thrill and joy in our hearts? Rex ran back to the leader dancing and with a broad grin on his face. I almost teared up at this point, thanking God for his grace and mercy and especially the boost of faith and morale for both of us. What I didn't know at that time was that this was only a prelude to something even greater.

Complete Healing in a Few Minutes

We finally settled into a hotel. The leader suggested we tour around a smaller shopping mall nearby as dinner was not until two hours later. I told Rex I was extremely tired and would like to rest instead of moving around. He was obedient and sympathetic.

So, we went back to the room and laid down on the bed. I felt the aches in the bones especially in the lower portion of my spine again. Judging from all the symptoms I had, the idea of being sick with flu was loud and clear. With the exhaustion, I asked Rex if he could pray for me, for God to heal me as soon as possible so that I could take care of him in the coming ten days and enjoy some fun time together. He answered with a firm yes, probably a result of the experience he had just had at the mall. That was huge for a ten-year-old. With faith and confidence in his voice, Rex asked God to heal his mom and enable his mom to recover as soon as possible. I closed my eyes and tears flew across my face. I relaxed and surrendered my whole body to God. Bit by bit, the aches in my lower back receded, then completely disappeared. I think this happened within just a few minutes. I told Rex I felt completely healed. All other symptoms of the flu were gone.

Rex was a bit surprised, but I was not. I knew God was greatly pleased by a child's sincere prayer. I was grateful beyond words that God healed me at such a critical time and gave Rex this springboard to greater faith and connection with him.

From that moment onward, my energy returned. I was able to join the other group members for dinner that night. I did not reach out for essential oils or other medical aid throughout the rest of the trip. I slept well and thrived and fully enjoyed my time with Rex. According to my experience and knowledge, it usually takes five or more days to be completely healed from a cold or the flu. And often, it ends up with coughing or phlegm. So, what can rightly explain this fast healing of mine in Portugal if not for the power of God? Let's sing hallelujah to the Lord!

CHAPTER 8

Signs and Directions to a Second Marriage

I have to say, my second marriage is a marriage endorsed and made possible by God because I saw so many signs, encouragement, and approval from all directions before I made the commitment to marry my husband, Steve Curtis, in 2015. Steve is a godly, loving, wise, humble, repentant, determined, efficient, and extremely positive person. He serves full-time as a minister in a church, which was the number one thing I asked God for when I prayed for a life partner.

I love Steve more and more as days pass, and I thank the Lord always for blessing me with a man like him. What else can you ask for when your husband is a pastor, a counselor, a chef, and an entertainer? Steve makes me laugh often, and I have laughed a lot more in the past five years with him than in the fifty years before our marriage.

According to the Chinese secular standard, Steve did not ring the bell for a desirable marriage at first sight though. Steve did not have his own house. (Most Hong Kong ladies would know what I mean here.) He rented a very small, humble apartment in Evergreen, Colorado, back in the time we dated. He did not have a lot of savings that could support two people's lives after retirement. (I was almost fifty by then and naturally looked for financial security.) He is handsome but balding, has a good build but short. And last but not least, he lived thousands of miles away from Hong Kong, in a territory that I did not have any knowledge of.

Praying for a Second Marriage

Around 2012, my dream of getting back with my ex-husband was crushed. My ex-husband confirmed over a brief meeting with me that he would not like to reestablish our relationship. I remember I almost knocked my glass of water off the table when I heard what he said.

This conversation, however, did not cause as much bitterness and grief as I had expected. For one or two years leading up to that conversation, I had worked hard on reconnecting with God and immersing in his words through BSF. Clearly, God's words had transformed me.

I was at peace with God and with myself. I knew I needed to move on, stop grabbing things for myself, and let God work on me. I prayed earnestly and constantly to God for a second chance to lead a married life that would serve him and glorify him. I still remember clearly that I prayed the same prayers while sitting in a Sunday worship. Looking at the altar, I asked God to give me a man who devoted full time to him and his people. I wanted to be a wife of a minister or pastor who served God wholeheartedly.

Confined to One Matching Site

Around that time, I was in a group of single lady friends who frequently got together to play badminton, have meals, and fellowship together. One of our topics was obviously dating and marriage. One lady highly recommended a matching website called E-Harmony. It is an international website that upholds Christian values. It is very well organized with lots of research data and statistics and offers sophisticated personality tests as well as highly secured matching services that would protect my identity and personal safety while giving me the best matches according to my criteria. I was convinced to try it, at least for half a year, and told myself if nothing came up, I would just forget about online dating.

After registering on E-Harmony in September of 2013, I went on to register on another local website so that I could have a greater chance of meeting a guy in Hong Kong. But alas, that local website rejected me on the ground that I was too discriminating and narrow by entering "devoted Christian" as a very important criterion. I was asked to change that into something like "spiritual" or else I would not be accepted.

As a Christian, I did not think I could compromise on this point. God says clearly in the Bible that it would be difficult for two persons of different beliefs to steer the same course.

> Do not be yoked together with unbelievers. For what do righteousness and wickedness have in common? Or what fellowship can light have with darkness? (2 Cor. 6:14 NIV)

There is always a reason that God closes some doors. So, I gave up registering on that local website and stayed solely on E-Harmony.

In merely a week, somebody on E-Harmony gave me a "wink." It was Steve Curtis. Steve looked good and sincere. He was a full-time minister at a church in Colorado. He had two daughters and was adventurous, as evidenced by his sky diving photos. Just a glance at his profile gave me a very positive feeling of him, so I responded to him right away.

During the following six months, we communicated with each other with eagerness and in great depth. I have to say, the challenging tests and Q and As stipulated by the website to guide us through showed that we were very much alike in terms of beliefs, values, life attitudes, and education level. However, this does not mean that things went smoothly without doubts and hesitation. I felt both excited and fearful in the first few weeks of communication. I was afraid of making mistakes and misreading God's guidance. What if I was wearing a pair of rosy glasses simply because I was too eager to have a life partner again? Why date somebody who is on the other side of the globe? After all the miscommunications with my ex-husband and the divorce, I had very little faith in my own perception and judgment of the opposite sex. I asked God for mercy and a big sign if he wanted me to continue the long-distance dating with Steve.

A Big Sign

I probably did not know what I was asking when I asked God for a big sign regarding Steve. I just felt I needed something very obvious from God as to whether or not this was the man he wanted me to marry.

God was humorous. On one public holiday in October of 2013, a few weeks after I met Steve online, my son Rex asked me to go shop for a pair of sports shoes with him. He suggested we go to Times Square in Causeway Bay, one of the most popular shopping districts in Hong Kong. He said there were shops there that sold the shoes he was looking for. It was a shopping mall that I had not visited for some time, and I needed to ask Rex which floor the store was on.

"Mom, it is on the seventh floor, the floor for sports," Rex said. I followed his instructions, and we chose to take the one and only elevator there instead of taking the escalator.

When the elevator door opened on the seventh floor, I could not help but exclaim, "Oh my goodness! God have mercy on me!"

Right in front of us was a big sign that read "STEVE." It was the first word of a shoe brand, but through the elevator door, I could only see "STEVE." I quickly deemed this big sign as a coincidence to make the experience less overwhelming for myself. *Well, I have never read any miracles from God that involved physical signs like an advertising banner, have I?* If God was really pointing me to Steve in that instant, using the word "sign" literally, he is surely a very humorous God.

But when a coincidence happens one after the other, they cannot be dubbed coincidence. That's what happened to me. Although I am still tempted to think of this big sign of Steve a mere coincidence, I could not dispel the idea that God was guiding me step by step to Steve. The numerous events that followed similarly showed huge and positive signals for an adventurous second marriage with a foreign pastor.

You might ask, did Steve perceive or experience positive signals and approval from God as well? I will leave this to him to answer this question. One thing I realized was that if we got married, I would be the one who would need to move since I was self-employed and more mobile. It would be a life-changing move. I needed obvious signals from God to boost my faith and courage to travel across the ocean.

Don't Grieve the Pastor

After six months of in-depth communications by e-mail, Skype, and text, along with a series of counseling sessions on divorce and remarriage conducted by Steve for me, we decided it was time to meet and see each other in person. Steve was a board member of New Horizons House (NHH), an aftercare facility in India that hosts and looks after girls rescued from sex trafficking and sex abuse. At that time, NHH was in its start-up stage and was looking for suitable locations to build the safe house. Some board members planned to go to India in February of 2014, and so Steve thought it was a good chance for him to stop over in Hong Kong for a few days to meet me.

Both of us knew it would be a critical meeting. We both understood if there was not any spark between us when we met, we would probably consider putting a stop to our dating.

I was nervous. I still remember the thirty or more minutes of waiting for Steve at the arrival hall of the Hong Kong Airport. It was like waiting for the announcement of public examination results. It seemed to me the whole world hinged on that.

Well, I have to be honest here. When Steve appeared, his look was not the most desirable according to the typical Chinese standard of tall and strong for men. He did look sweet and handsome as he appeared on Skype, but he was much shorter than I expected. He dressed in the most casual, comfortable manner. He carried a heavy leather bag of books that pulled one side of his shoulder down while pulling a big old-fashioned nylon luggage with his hand on the other side.

However, he was very good-spirited, gentle, polite, and cheerful. With all my knowledge and understanding of him now as a wife, I would certainly say the score of his character and personality should more than offset the short and small figure. But given the huge pressure of a life decision at that time, any slight deviation from perfection would appear to be a "warning."

Steve arrived in the evening, so the first thing we did was to settle down in his hotel. He treated me with a lot of respect, and we had a really good in-depth talk before I left. On my way home that night, I felt very divided. I kept talking to myself and praying to the Lord. *Steve is a very godly man, which is rare in this world. The figure should be second. Is height really that important to me?* I prayed, "God please help me to be less shallow. Change my perception. Reveal your will for me. I don't want to feel uncomfortable with anything if he is the man you ordain for me. Shouldn't I feel super excited and happy and satisfied if he is the one? God, if he is not the one, please intercede and take him away."

My prayers continued into my usual personal quiet time before bed. I took up *Our Daily Bread* [5] and turned to the page for the day of February 16, 2014. Having just asked God to take Steve away, what appeared in front of my eyes was like a big hit on my head! "Why Cause Grief?" was the title of the passage. Reflecting on the passage from Hebrews 13:17–19, the writer said,

---

5 . Our Daily Bread. Grand Rapids: Our Daily Bread Ministries, 2014.

Pastors make an easy target for criticism. Every week they are on display, carefully explaining God's Word, challenging us toward Christ-like living. But sometimes we look to find things to criticize. It's easy to overlook all the good things a pastor does and focus on our personal opinions.... Like all of us, our pastors are not perfect.... Our pastor is responsible for guiding us spiritually. We should want that burden to be joyous, not grievous. The passage (of Hebrews) indicates that causing grief for the pastor "would be of no benefit." (Dave Branon)

Of course, the passage was talking about the need for church members to support and protect their pastors, not about dating or matching. But it resonated with me. I immediately knelt to ask God for forgiveness. I asked God to forgive the little faith I had and to change my perception and feeling about height.

"Perception and prejudice are not something easy to alter," is a saying in Chinese. My experience this time proved this wrong though. The next morning, we met early. I looked at him and felt perplexed. I was wrong; he was not that short. He was taller than me by at least two inches. I could not believe my eyes.

"Oh my God, my Lord, you take care of trivial issues even like this?" I was astonished by God. I was ashamed of my request for a change of perception. I begged for forgiveness for my stupid concern.

God satisfied my selfish request anyway in this case. His mercy was so huge. He has been obvious, and he was then even more obvious. Steve and I had a great time getting to know each other even better during this visit. I introduced him to my sister and brother-in-law over dinner. We met briefly with the minister of my church and had an hour-long session with my counselor, Teresa. All went well, and everybody found him decent and trustworthy. I started to think of going to the US to visit and find out more about this potential life partner.

Lost and Found

With great anticipation for our future, I said good-bye to Steve at the Hong Kong Airport. His visit was brief, just two days, but it seemed like we had already done a lot of talking and walking and eating and meeting with people together. I had a lot of precious photos of us on my phone and could not help but go through the photos again and again on my way home. I took the Airport Express (an express train) to downtown Central, and after getting off, I walked ten minutes to a bus terminal to take a minibus home. There was a line, as usual, and when I was finally able to get onto the minibus, I quickly grabbed a window seat. I knew it would be another thirty minutes' ride.

Having settled myself for a while on the minibus, I planned to indulge myself in the photos again. I went deep into my bag to look for my phone, but I could not find it. I searched all over my bag. No! It wasn't there. I started to panic and looked under my seat. I looked under the seat in front of me and the one at the back. People started to notice my panicky search and my distress, and they started to help look under their seats as well. There was no sign of my phone on the whole minibus. By then, the minibus had come to the terminal. The driver was so kind that he allowed me to stay on the bus after everybody got off to do another search again. We both came to a point that we thought we had to give up. With great disappointment, I figured I must have lost the phone before boarding the minibus.

I could not hold my tears when I finally opened the door to my place. I rushed into my room and prayed to my Lord, "God, if this is a relationship you delight in, please let me find my phone and thus all the photos of us. Are you showing me that I have been mistaken about the relationship by taking away all the photos of us? Forgive my little faith, God, and please grant me another miracle to show me your approval."

I knew immediately I was unreasonable to make this request. How could I, a created being, request the Creator to reveal his will for me in a way that I desired? Why was my faith so weak? Hadn't God already shown me time and time again that he had opened doors for us? Besides, why should my interpretation of circumstances be so rigid—as if God did not make something happen, then he did not approve; or if he did not deliver me from this trouble, then he did not care; or if he did not continue to show me miracles, then my past experiences with him were all wrong.

The words "even if God does not [deliver]" in Daniel 3:18 reminded me that I needed to have faith in him and have faith in my past experiences with him even if my phone was not found.

Rising from my prayers and tears, I suddenly had the idea that I might have lost my phone during the train journey. A beam of light flooded through my heart, and I suddenly felt hopeful. I could not explain this sudden beam of hope. I quickly looked for the number of the lost and found department of the train company and made a call. After a few transfers, the party on the other side of the line asked me to describe the appearance and model number of my phone. I did. Then he asked me if I have another phone at home to make a call to my lost phone. I forgot how I got another phone at that moment (maybe it was from my maid at home), but once I dialed my phone number, I heard the sound of ringing, so familiar and endearing, on the other side of the line.

I found my phone! After making an impassioned appeal to the Lord, and after just a few phone calls, I heard the ringing of my phone on the other side of the line. We can say it was luck, but my experience told me it was another miracle from God. He was so merciful to a timid person like me. He knew my fear. He knew the move across the ocean was like facing Goliath. And he granted me again his obvious signal for continuing to date Steve.

Blessings from People and Circumstances

What followed in the next two years was more communication and face-to-face meetings with Steve. God opened doors in almost every situation to enable us to see each other as much as possible before marriage.

To visit Steve in the US, the first big hurdle was to apply for a US travel visa. As a divorced, single woman, and as a Chinese, applying for a US visa was not that easy. (The US government is especially suspicious of single Chinese women trying to stay in the US illegally or to immigrate through fake marriages.) Apart from filling in and submitting lengthy forms, I was also required to go for a face-to-face interview at the US embassy in Hong Kong.

That morning, on my way out to the interview, I realized I had forgotten to print out three months' worth of bank statements and some other financial proof. I could not understand how this could have happened given the fact that I was so eager to obtain the visa. But it was too late to do that by then. I quickly prayed to God when I closed the door behind me and asked for mercy again. I quietly assured myself that if God approved the dating, he would let me get the visa. I was so uncertain yet so certain at the same time.

To my relief, the interviewer did not ask for any financial supporting documents, and our conversation lasted less than five minutes. It was a light-hearted interview. The interviewer said Colorado was a gorgeous place surrounded by mountains and wished me all the best for my trip. I was approved for the visa right away.

I did not know much about Denver, Colorado. It was like exploring a new territory. Denver is dubbed the mile-high city because it is located a mile higher than sea level on a plateau. It is not unusual that you will suffer high altitude syndrome with symptoms such as breathlessness, headache, nausea, insomnia, and so on upon your first arrival. I was so fortunate on my first visit that

I was not bothered by any symptoms. I was actually not aware of this issue until I found my stomach a little bit upset one morning. But apart from that one morning, everything was fine. I loved the openness, the sunshine (not the UV light though), and the brightness. I was amazed by the extensive and magnificent mountains. I love nature, and so I quickly fell in love with the place. Besides, the church where Steve ministered was a loving and supportive community. I became good friends with many church members in a short time even before getting married.

We started to have thoughts of getting married, but since Rex was just twelve in 2014, and he lived with me, we did not think we should get married until he became more mature and independent. I love Rex and he is a priority in my life. I would do anything for him, including delaying my marriage.

Rex was studying at an international school, and many students of that school considered studying overseas as a natural option when they were at Grade 9 (around age fourteen or fifteen). Rex's dad actually mentioned that and suggested I make a plan for Rex in advance.

One night in the first quarter of 2014, Rex told me he wanted to go study abroad as soon as possible. I asked him why. He gave me some personal reasons, which I could completely understand. Rex was a very talented boy and extremely skilled in soccer. But he was relatively hyperactive and did not fit in very well with the strict classroom rules in Hong Kong. Besides, Rex and his peers spent a lot of time on online chats and games, and I had been struggling with him to pull him away from these temptations, which I believed could eventually develop into an addiction.

I discussed Rex's desires with his dad, and we started to search for opportunities. We even brought Rex to a counselor and psychologist to check on his emotional stability and resilience to make sure he could handle the overseas study.

The experts recommended that it might be good for Rex to go earlier if that was his future path anyway. They said people of a younger age adapted much faster and better to new environments, and it would be a way to avoid the development of an internet addiction if he could be trained to live with a strict routine and discipline in the boarding house.

In September of that year, Rex was admitted to Grade 7 at an international full boarding school in the UK. Everything was surprisingly smooth and so well provided for. I did not even have to look for a guardian for Rex because a good friend's relative just happened to live near Rex's school, and she was ready and eager to help. She was a very loving mom of a child with special needs. She was caring, supportive, communicative, and extremely efficient. It gave us great peace of mind to have her as Rex's guardian.

Leaving Rex behind in the UK was, of course, very heartbreaking for me. I talked with Rex over the phone almost every day in the first week of his boarding. We both cried a lot. But God's grace was more abundant than I could have imagined. Within just two weeks at the boarding school, Rex had blended in well with the community. He even became a member of the school soccer team. He forgot about appointments with me over Skype. There were always friends next to him when we talked, and so he needed to cut the conversations short. I missed him a lot but also felt extremely glad for him.

So, Steve and I started to plan for our marriage. Since Rex would return to Hong Kong three times a year for his term breaks, I asked Steve if he would agree to me leaving the US three times a year to take care of Rex in Hong Kong. After all, he was still not yet an adult, and so he was a priority in my care list. Steve agreed without any hesitation. Our wedding ceremony took place on April 18, 2015, in Colorado, then we had a banquet for my family in Hong Kong on August 8 the same year. Rex gave me his blessing by attending the banquet in Hong Kong. He even led the family to sing a song that night. I am deeply grateful to Rex for accepting my second marriage.

Both Rex and I have started a new exciting journey in our lives since 2014, and I know deep in my heart that it was God who had made everything work together for our good. He had removed all potential obstacles and instituted the right people and circumstances to bring me next to Steve. There are, of course, times when I miss my family and friends in Hong Kong, but in general, I enjoy my life in the US more than expected. I feel well supported emotionally and spiritually. Although the US government still calls me an "alien" at the time I am writing this book, I feel I have been living in the US for a long time.

Car Accident—
Blessing in a Curse

I have never had the experience of being close to a big car crash, not to mention being involved in one, until the morning of November 26, 2017. It was a bright, sunny Sunday, and I was on my way to church in the US. My usual route was to go farther down a lane where there is an intersection with traffic lights that enable easier turning onto the main road, but I took a different route that morning, as I saw that there was little traffic on the main road.

I was not driving fast or in a hurry at all. When I reached the junction, I stopped, looked to the left, then to the right. I figured I could enter the road when I saw there was no car from the left and only one car far away from the right. So, I charged onto the road ready to turn left. In a fraction of a second, before I could realize what had happened, I heard a deafening bang from the left.

My car's left front was completely smashed. At the same time, I saw big and small pieces of metallic fragments flying in front of the windshield to the right.

And then everything became quiet, still, and blurry. I was stunned and confused. I could not understand why this had happened. I did not see any car coming from the left. I was so shocked that I did not even realize the airbag was already blown up against my chest and my face. I looked at the smoky bright light in front of and around me. I saw a man coming out from a car farther down to the right, and he pointed at me while shouting out some words.

I figured to myself, *So, this is an accident. My car is smashed and damaged and no longer fit for driving.*

I was more concerned about the car than myself because I did not feel any pain anywhere on my body. Then I saw a woman running toward my car. She waved and told me she was a nurse and could help me. She asked me to pull the handbrake and turn off the engine. *Wow, how had I not realized that the car engine was not turned off at all?* I questioned myself, feeling weak on all levels. The nurse asked me a few more questions and touched my forehead to make sure I was OK. She then said she could pray for me. It was at this time that I knew I was in good hands.

Within seconds, a police car and ambulance arrived. I realized I needed to call my husband, so I handed my phone to the policewoman who was checking on me. Some first-aiders put a brace around my neck in case I had a bone fracture somewhere along my spine. They then helped me get out of the car and move into the ambulance. My husband arrived while I was being escorted into the ambulance. He took pictures of my car and liaised with the police and the other driver after the ambulance left.

Lying on a stretcher in the emergency room, with my neck brace still on, I could not turn my head but could hear that my husband and a few members of the church came in to check on me. It was then that tears ran down my face. I was not in pain, nor devastated in any way physically. But I could not control the tears that flowed from an internal wave of shock and grief. I was shocked, as I did not anticipate the accident, even to the last second. My husband said the car that hit me was white in color, and I might have been blind to it when bright sunlight shone on it. I grieved the loss of my car. My car was, in insurance terms, totaled. I could not recognize my car from the pictures at all. The front was badly crushed and looked as if there was a wide-open mouth with black and broken teeth inside.

A medical attendant told my husband that there were no external wounds at all. There was no bruise, no scratch, nor any impression that could possibly be incurred by the airbag or safety belt. I was then urged to go through some CT scans to make sure there were no internal wounds. They scanned my whole upper body and found no twist, crack, or fracture. Everything was fine, except for a shadow on my thyroid.

Shadow on the Thyroid

This was a huge surprise. As per information from the doctor, thyroidal nodes or tumors do not usually present any symptoms, and seldom would people go for a scan of the thyroid unless they have symptoms of hormonal imbalance. The doctor advised me to check out my thyroid as soon as possible to make sure it was not something malignant.

As I did not have any medical insurance in the US, which was way too expensive for us, I consulted a specialist in Hong Kong when I went back to the city for Christmas that year. The shadow on the thyroid was relatively big, and I was required to go through a biopsy to make sure it was not cancer. Waiting for the results of the biopsy, which was available only a few days later, was tormenting. My worries and anxiety were immense. I prayed day and night for peace and healing. I made an effort to remember all the miracles and blessings I had experienced in the previous years. I thanked God for the peculiar car accident that alerted me to the thyroid issue and bargained with him for a positive outcome so that I could continue to work hand in hand with my husband to serve God and his people.

On the day my report was supposed to be out, I called the clinic instead of waiting for their call. The nurse on the other side of the line asked me to wait. Every second during that wait was like a thousand years. Finally, the nurse came back with the biopsy report and told me the nodules formed by calcification were *not* malignant. However, the nodules were big and numerous. Close monitoring of my thyroid was important because there was still the possibility that the cells could mutate. No medication was needed for the time being. I was advised to schedule scanning and a check-up once every year.

What a big relief for me and Steve.

I emerged unhurt, with not even a scratch, from the car accident. God made use of the accident to point me to something that I was totally unaware of. It was something deep down in my tissue that I needed to take care of before things turned foul. I would surely not have gone for a scan as not a single symptom of any kind had ever presented itself. In hindsight, I could say that the accident helped uncover a bomb before it exploded. It was a blessing in disguise.

CHAPTER 10

I Heard Him Whisper in My Ear

History of Panic Attacks and Insomnia

I suffered from panic attacks and insomnia after my father's sudden death from a heart attack, then my sister's traffic accident in 1998. I was running my own public relations firm at that time, and my stress level was already high. These traumatic events only shot it up further to go beyond my emotional threshold. I experienced severe shaking, palpitations, sweating, and constant insomnia. I was diagnosed with panic attacks, and I needed to take medication (mainly tranquilizers and sleeping pills) for more than a year to remain in control.

Then, thanks to various alternative therapies including aromatherapy, I was able to quit the medicine and get back on track. For almost twenty years, there were rarely any relapses, and if there were, they were so mild that I could deal with them within a few days through a combination of natural therapies or a mild dose of medicine. All I had was muscle tension or occasional sleep issues due to frequent flying and jet lag. I could barely remember the shaky sensations, the palpitations, or the shortness of breath. I thought panic attacks were history for me.

Relapse

After getting remarried in 2015, I lived mainly in the US and returned to Hong Kong three times a year to spend time with my son during his holidays and term breaks (Christmas, Easter, and summer). The summer stay in Hong Kong in 2018 was a particularly long one—two whole months. I had many hours of teaching and numerous orders from customers for essential oil blends during that period, in addition to cooking at least two meals a day for my son, meeting family and friends, and studying herbal medicine online. I did not realize that I had harbored a lot of stress until I flew back to the US in early September and experienced great difficulty in readjusting to the time difference. This had not been the case in the previous few years; I could overcome jet lag within a few days, and I took pride in it.

As an aromatherapist, not being able to sleep well was a big deal to me. I taught people how to relax their bodies and minds. I have a lot of resources on hand to promote sleep naturally. It was a shame not to be able to apply to myself what I preached. I felt like a complete failure. With these thoughts and a perfectionist's mindset creeping in, I made every effort to force myself to get well. But the irony is that sleep cannot be forced to take place. The more you want to sleep, the less you will be able to. Sleep comes only when you surrender yourself instead of being conscious of yourself. So, I set myself up for failure by being impatient and overly conscious. And this started the domino effect of disaster.

For over two weeks, I was not able to adjust. I either could not fall asleep or woke up too often. I went for acupuncture treatment. I took Chinese medicine. I even reached out to my own standby stock of tranquilizers in the hope of a quick fix. Insufficient sleep had probably robbed me of peace and sanity. The tranquilizer did give me some deep sleep, but it was just a quick fix that caused more damage than good.

Then one night, the palpitations and shaky sensation that I had experienced twenty years ago returned. Although it was not a full-blown attack, it was a frightening experience. The fear of having to go through the symptoms of panic attacks again was distressing. My husband wrapped his arms around me and prayed for me. My body calmed down and warmed up a bit, but I still could not sleep through the night.

I finally went to see a western family doctor. She gave me some sleeping pills in the hope of putting me to sleep and thus easing the panicky feelings. It did not work. Even a sleeping pill did not give me a peaceful, long sleep. I was in great despair. I lived like a zombie for many days.

It occurred to us that I needed the help of a psychiatrist who could prescribe the right kind of medicine. Seeing a psychiatrist in the US costs a fortune. Besides, I have no insurance to cover this kind of medical expense. Fortunately, my husband happened to meet a Christian psychiatrist a few months before my return. She was willing to see me at a discounted fee, but I did not have a very good feeling about her in the beginning. She looked very young. Her online registration system was down slightly before the first session, and it took us almost half a session's time to finish the questionnaire. Without a lot of trust, I doubted if I could benefit a lot from her treatment.

I started to think about going back to Hong Kong to consult the psychiatrist who treated me twenty years ago. It was not an easy decision at all. A lot had to be rescheduled if I was really going to go back to Hong Kong at that time. I had enrolled in an aromatherapy conference that would take place in mid-October, which was a few weeks later. And there would be a trip to visit NHH in India in November. Steve, who was vice president of this charitable project, was eager to go and wanted me to join him.

"I Will Help You."

One afternoon during this period of great distress and uncertainty, I was lying in bed with my eye mask on and earplugs in both ears. I was lying on my right side, with my right ear pressing against the pillow. Instead of struggling to sleep, I was busy making plans inside my brain for a special trip back to Hong Kong. I thought of withdrawing my enrollment and getting a refund from the conference. I planned to fly direct to India from Hong Kong instead of from the US.

While I was still in deep thought about all the possibilities, I heard a voice speak into my left ear.

"I will help you," a male tenor voice said in a very gentle but firm manner.

I could even feel the vibration it created in my left ear. I was startled and confused but also elated and comforted at the same time. The message was so reassuring. It brought so much hope. But who was it that was speaking to me? Was it the Spirit of God? My first reaction was to thank God for his assurance and promise. Then came all the doubts and the thoughts of other possibilities. Was it my husband? Or was it just my own imagination or hallucination?

No, it could not have been my imagination. I was thinking about the trip back to Hong Kong at that time. My brain could not spare a second for imagination. And it was quite impossible that I heard Steve's voice so clearly while he was out in the living room. My bedroom door was closed, and I had my earplugs on. The voice penetrated deep into my left ear.

I told Steve this extraordinary experience. He confirmed he had not spoken anything to me that afternoon. He had not thought of saying the four words to anybody.

I thanked God again and asked him to take charge of my situation, just as he had promised. I put down my plans to go back to Hong Kong and waited with anticipation for new developments in my healing journey. The hope inside me was so strong that I felt less agitated even when I was not able to sleep at night. The creator of the universe had spoken to me and had given me a promise! With God's help, I should be able to overcome whatever obstacles are in front of me. I trust that everything is possible in him and that he has my best interest in mind.

A Positive Turn of Events

What was strange was that when I trusted God's plan, my perception of my psychiatrist also started to change. She had, in fact, taken a very natural approach, which was exactly what I preached. The medication she prescribed was mild and nonaddictive. She advised me to practice meditation, drink herbal tea, and be consistent and intentional with all these practices. I believe it was me who was prejudiced and unappreciative.

Since then, I gladly followed everything I was asked to do, and in less than a week after the voice, my sleep was greatly improved. My strength was restored, and I felt more confident with all the activities that had been planned.

So, instead of going back to Hong Kong and canceling my trip to the aromatherapy conference in Salt Lake City, I flew there and stayed there for three nights. Apart from attending the conference, which was the best one that I had ever attended so far, I traveled around the city and enjoyed a lot of sites and conversations with strangers. I immersed myself totally in the joy of learning and networking with other therapists. Last but not least, I reaped a whole bag of souvenirs and samples from generous exhibitors. "Abundance" was the word I used to describe to others this particular trip. God had changed the course of events to enable me to enjoy such abundance in life.

As for the trip to India, I had had concerns and hesitations right from the start of talking and planning for it, even before the relapse. NHH is situated in a very remote area in India. Transportation can take a whole day, and the living facilities can be extremely primitive. Besides, we were warned of the possibilities of infections and diseases. Given my poor physical and mental condition after the relapse, I had thought of not going at all.

But because of God's encouraging words and my rapid recovery, I was more than willing and able to join Steve and another couple for this adventure. To everybody's surprise, I had been healthy and energetic throughout the whole trip. I survived the long bumpy rides, the less than desirable living conditions, and the hot and humid climate. I slept well and even dozed off many times (which I seldom had the privilege of in the past) while traveling. I enjoyed most of the meals. I took the courage to sit next to the driver and took a lot of pictures of the busy, disorganized, and dangerous traffic (which was a mix of modern vehicles, tricycles, motorbikes, trucks, and cows). But most important of all, a fire was kindled inside my heart to help the girls who were hosted in the safe house. It was not just sympathy and care, but rather an urge and passion to do something for them.

I went directly back to Hong Kong from India after the trip. I could not forget all the beautiful faces at NHH. Although Steve was vice president of NHH, I had never thought of volunteering for the ministry. I supported Steve, but I did not see how I could contribute. Now I felt completely different. I thought of ways to show my care and to encourage each of the girls. I asked for their birthdays and sent out cards and gifts. I developed photos and created an album for the girls and the staff members. I started to ask for opportunities to give presentations on this charitable cause and solicit donations and support. God amazingly opened doors for me. I gave my first slide presentation of NHH at the worship service of a Chinese church. They allowed me to set up a booth at the reception, and on that day alone, I was able to collect a significant amount of cash donations.These donations were enough to support a girl at NHH for half a year.

Great things happened one after another. Every time I returned to Hong Kong since then, I was given opportunities to speak and raise funds for NHH. It was like a tap being turned on. As per the NHH president's report in January of 2020, the funds we raised in Hong Kong accounted for fifteen percent of the total donations received throughout 2019.

All these started with the four words I heard.

"I will help you," said the Spirit of God.

I was helped to bless others.

Further Reassurance

Having gone through the healing and all the sub-sequent encouraging events, I felt confident and brave enough to share my story with other Christians. But not everybody believed that the voice was from God.

A friend of mine, who had a PhD in neurological science, said that the voice was probably a hallucination.

"You had insomnia those days, and it is not uncommon for those who have insomnia for a few days to experience hallucinations," he said.

"But how about the words that I heard? It was positive and unlikely to come from my brain when I was depressed." I asked.

"Well, it was consistent with your usual route of thinking though. You believe in God, and you expect God to help. Our brain works in mysterious ways, and you never know what data you have stored up in your unconscious mind and what would be retrieved at times when you have little control over your brain. Insomnia could cause hallucination," he said with an air of certainty.

This conversation weighed heavily on me and dampened my enthusiasm about witnessing to others.

I started to doubt my judgment and memory. Was it my own creation? Was everything simply a psychological effect instead of the result of a miracle? I asked God for his revelation and confirmation.

"Lord, please help my little faith. I don't want to tell a story that is not true. Assure me that you have spoken to me," I prayed.

I booked another session with my psychiatrist in the US to obtain her professional opinion.

"According to my experience and past documentation, there are a few typical characteristics of hallucinations. First, either visually or auditorily, hallucinations are usually recurrent. Did you have other episodes of hallucinations prior to or after that?" she asked.

"No, I've never had any other episode," I replied. "What are the other characteristics?"

"The content of hallucinations is usually negative, e.g., a voice warning you of possible attacks or commanding you to jump off the verandah, and so on. I have never heard of anything that is so positive and encouraging such as 'I will help you.' That's very rare, if not totally impossible," she answered. "And because the messages are usually negative, the consequences or subsequent events are also negative and even tragic. Consider all the positive events that happened after you heard the voice; I would not say it is hallucination."

As a Christian psychiatrist, my doctor believes in miracles. She seemed to be happy with her analysis and even said it was very likely that God spoke to me.

I was overjoyed! Despite my little faith, God was patient with me. He gave me a chance to see my experience in a new light and reassured me through a human authority.

A few months later, I saw the following verse while reading the book of Isaiah in my personal devotion:

> *For I am the Lord your God*
> *who takes hold of your right hand*
> *and says to you, do not fear;*
> *I will help you. (Isa. 41:13 NIV)*

Wow! Here are the four words: "I will help you." It was the first time I read through the book of Isaiah and paid close attention to this verse in English. It is amazing to see that God used the same vocabulary and spoke in the same tone and manner thousands of years ago! God is the God of the past, the present, and the future, and he never changes. He spoke in the past. He still speaks today.

Part 4: Reflections

CHAPTER 11

What I Have Learned

I have learned a lot about human nature and in particular about myself through all these spiritual experiences over the past decade. I also learned a lot about God and his unchanging character and love. I am in debt to him and to all my Christian family for all that has happened to me and nourished me into the person I am now. There is so much to talk about when I think about God and my transformation. But what I have chosen to talk about below is something that I think is significant, something people will be interested in and would like to discuss and dig into deeper. I hope my following reflections will stimulate thoughts, comments, and responses from my readers.

The Power of a Child's Heart

When I experienced immediate healing after my son prayed for me (see Chapter 7), I realized the importance and power of a child's prayer. I have heard stories of how a child's prayer changed the lives of people and even the course of events. I know God loves children and sees them as especially precious. But does this mean that God will bend down and listen more to a child's prayer than the same from an adult?

Children are weaker and more vulnerable than adults. They have little to lean on for survival and will sincerely look up to adults for almost everything they need. They seldom play politics or have an agenda when they interact with others. Sometimes they can be so transparent or straightforward in speech that they can embarrass us.

God loves children probably because of such sincerity, humility, honesty, and transparency. They are more likely to be "the pure in heart" and "the poor in spirit" whom God says will inherit the kingdom of heaven.

> Let the little children come to me and do not
> hinder them. The kingdom of God belongs to
> such as these. (Mark 10:14 NIV)

Blessed are the poor in spirit, for theirs is the kingdom of heaven. (Matt. 5:3 NIV)

Blessed are the pure in heart, for they will see God. (Matt. 5:8 NIV)

The pure in heart. That's the point.

I strongly believe that when any person prays with a child's heart for anything that is in God's will, God will be especially moved. It is important to allow children to learn to talk to God and walk with him. It is of even greater importance that we learn to be like children and be pure and humble in heart.

Surely God is good . . . to those who are pure in heart. (Ps. 73:1 NIV)

Spiritual Sensitivity

It has not been easy for me to share my supernatural experiences with others. People's responses varied, but mostly, they were not very encouraging. The suspicion on their faces and the dead air that followed my sharing often made me feel odd and embarrassed.

I can understand why it is so difficult to believe in supernatural events and miracles, even among Christians. It can be disturbing to know that things can happen not following the law of nature that we are so familiar and comfortable with. We, throughout our whole lives, are trained to embrace and believe in science, which has, indeed, helped resolve many mysteries that had once baffled our ancestors. We feel relieved when things can be explained in a way we can master and understand. We care about people's opinions of us and don't want to be the odd person out. And worst of all, some miracles have turned out to be fake stories made up by people out of selfish motives. This reinforces our skepticism about miracles and leaves us feeling that we have been deceived.

But as Christians, if we believe in God, who created the universe from nothing, isn't it logical and natural to also believe in supernatural events? Shouldn't we believe in the existence of a world that is beyond our five senses and beyond our control?

And when God grants us what we pray for, such as healing or deliverance from a grave situation, would we truly believe that it is the work of God, or we would rather explain it away as coincidence, luck, or the blessing of science and technology? What is the point of praying if we refuse to believe in God's intervention?

I believe we can all see miracles if we are not suppressing our spiritual sensitivity with explanations like luck, illusions, misperceptions, or coincidence. I am not saying that there is no luck, illusion, misperception, or coincidence. There is. But I believe there are also heavenly miracles. Spiritual sensitivity needs to be nourished. The noise outside and inside of us often drowns out the whisper of the Spirit. God is powerful, but God's voice doesn't have to be loud or frightening. A lot of passages in the Bible describe God's voice as a gentle whisper:

> *Be still, and know that I am God... (Ps. 46:10a NIV)*

> *After the earthquake came a fire, but the* LORD *was not in the fire. And after the fire came a gentle whisper [from God]. (1 Kings 19:12 NIV)*

I am not well trained in the practice of meditation and spirituality, so I cannot give concrete suggestions in this area. The fact that I heard God's voice and saw his intervention is as big of a surprise to me as it is to you. I really cannot remember what I had done consciously and specifically each time to be granted a miracle, except for, maybe, sincerely praying to our almighty Lord for forgiveness, help, and mercy. In most cases, my emotional state was one that was completely broken down, and my mental state completely emptied and opened up to God before I experienced his miracles.

My sacrifice, O God, is a broken spirit; a broken and contrite heart you, God, will not despise. (Ps. 51:17 NIV)

But one thing I know for sure: once we are able to see one miracle, we will see more.

Miracles Do Not Necessarily Lead to Faith

Miracles do not always lead people to trust and believe in God. This is a very sad piece of news. I read this in the Bible, and I experienced this myself in many instances. In both Old and New Testament times, the Israelites had been forgetful, ungrateful, and skeptical all along, despite the many miracles they had experienced.

They [the Israelites] refused to listen and failed to remember the miracles you [God] performed among them. They became stiff-necked and, in their rebellion, appointed a leader in order to return to their slavery. (Neh. 9:17 NIV)

When our ancestors were in Egypt, they gave no thought to your [God's] miracles; they did not remember your many kindnesses, and they rebelled by the sea, the Red Sea. (Ps. 106:7 NIV)

Isn't this alarming? Not long after they had seen the separation of the Red Sea, which was a huge display of God's omnipotence and sovereignty, and had walked past the dried-up sea bed with their own feet, the Israelites forgot and refused to trust in God's power and loving-kindness!

While my jaw dropped each time I read these passages, I was also convicted. Deep inside my heart, I know that I have done the same thing. I doubted my overall perception of miracles that I or others had experienced. I forgot what God had miraculously done for me in the past when I suffered illnesses, misfortunes, or faced obstacles and attacks. I took God's miracles for granted and queried him when I heard no answers. I am not very different from the Israelites described in the Bible.

God pointed out clearly that it was faith that brought people to his presence and the inheritance of eternal life.

> For it is by grace you have been saved, through faith—and this is not from yourselves, it is the gift of God. (Eph. 2:8 NIV)

> And without faith it is impossible to please God, because anyone who comes to him must believe that he exists and that he rewards those who earnestly seek him. (Heb. 11:6 NIV)

> *But as I [Jesus] told you, you have seen me and*
> *still you do not believe. (John 6:36 NIV)*

It is not miracles that bring people to God. It is faith.

In Greek, the word "miracle" means "signs." A miracle can be a sign or pointer that leads to belief and faith and can help build up our faith. But only if we allow it to.

Miracles are probably not a strategy that God uses to draw us to him. Jesus performed numerous miracles before and after his death and resurrection. He healed the sick, raised the dead, turned water into wine, cast out demons, and so on. A lot of people were amazed and attracted to follow him. But at the same time, a lot doubted and were disturbed and even angered by his deeds, which eventually led to his crucifixion.

It was not the aim or focus of Jesus's ministry to heal and perform miracles. These were the results of his mercy and compassion. His focus was on our ultimate salvation and reconciliation with God. He died on the cross to cleanse us from our sins so that we can be right with our holy Father and have eternal life. This gift of salvation is already extended to every one of us, just waiting for a step of faith on our part to accept it.

CHAPTER 12

When There Is No Miracle

Given what I have shared above, that God never intends to use miracles to draw us to him and that miracles can be a sign that leads to faith only if we allow them to, it is sensible to say that we don't need to have miracles to believe in God and to have faith in him.

But we all long to see miracles. When our loved ones are sick or dying, when we face an insurmountable financial burden and might soon go bankrupt or become homeless, when there are widespread riots or wars between nations and tribes, when a pandemic brings the whole world to a standstill and the number of deaths keeps rising, we wholeheartedly pray and plead and beg God to turn things around.

When suffering is rampant and things do not turn around miraculously, what can we do? Is there a way to move God's hands and heart to make miracles happen? I don't have an answer to this. I have seen juvenile delinquents becoming Christians after years of consistent and unfailing prayers on the part of the parents. I have read how a doctor heard and immediately followed the prompt of the Holy Spirit to give an electric shock to a man and bring him back to life from death. I have seen complete, miraculous healing from terminal cancer. There is no formula. We have not discovered one formula that will move God's fingers or change God's mind to bring a miracle. And I think, if there was one, God is no longer God but only our vending machine.

Why does God grant miracles in some cases and not in others? We have a prayer group in our church that collects prayer requests and prays constantly for people who are suffering on different levels. Throughout the years, we have seen cases of rapid healing as well as those of continuous sickness or even death. Is God then showing favor to some over others? Surely not! "God does not show favoritism" (Rom 2:11 NIV). The Bible tells stories of family tragedies that are a direct or indirect result of parental favoritism. James explicitly said that favoritism is a sin:

> Yes indeed, it is good when you obey the royal law as found in the Scriptures: "Love

your neighbor as yourself." But if you favor
some people over others, you are committing a
sin. You are guilty of breaking the law. (James
2:8–9 NLT)

God is a fully just and loving God. The only one he
has treated unfairly was himself. He loves us to the extent of laying aside his divinity to identify with us sinners so that he could live, suffer, and die for our sins on
earth. His redemption is a free gift to everybody. He has
every one of us in mind and has planned the most perfect finale for every individual. We might not be able to
appreciate it at the moment, but we will, eventually.

God knows what is best for us. We tend to equate
miracles with blessings, and blessings with wealth,
health, success, achievement, and so on. But sometimes
what we think is good turns out to be a curse, and a curse,
a blessing. We don't have the panoramic view of history
to tell which tiny piece in our life puzzle will match well
with another to eventually create the most beautiful and
perfect picture in the will of God. When things turn sour,
become disastrous, or no hope is in sight, have faith that
it is not yet the end.

God is sovereign. Miracles or no miracles, it is not up
to us at all. Everything is in his hands, and he knows everything from the beginning to the end. He orchestrates

all events to fulfill his will and eternal purposes. He is all-wise and good. He can even make use of something evil to transform us to achieve his will.

If we truly believe in God and see God as he is and not as we wish he would be, we would not question God when there is no miracle. Can we ask the Sovereign Lord to act according to our wishes? We don't have the right or power to map things out for him or question him when he does not follow our plan.

Jesus said those who have not seen him yet believe in him are blessed:

> Then Jesus told him [Thomas], "Because you have seen me, you have believed; blessed are those who have not seen and yet have believed."
> (John 20:29 NIV)

In a similar way, I think those who have not seen or experienced a miracle yet still persevere in faith despite unfavorable circumstances are truly blessed in God's eyes. What is better than a "well done" from our almighty God? Not long ago, I came across a message on FaceBook that said:

> Grapes must be crushed to make wine. Diamonds form under pressure....Whenever you feel crushed, under pressure,

pressed, or in darkness, you're in a powerful place of transformation. Trust the
process. (Lalah Delia)

"Trust the process." Maybe this sounds cruel and inhuman to you, that sometimes our God allows suffering in our lives in order to train, grow and refine us; that sometimes he appears to be blind to tragic events for reasons we have yet to grasp and understand. But to be blunt, we all deserve death and eternal hopelessness. Instead, God went through the most torturing and agonizing death on our behalf. He promises us his company through the darkest valley and a glorious future when we trust in him. For me, recalling what God has done in the past and meditating on his love and perfect character help dispel my doubts and instill faith and trust in him..

Still, I can understand the challenges and questions we all have in this regard. Suffering is such a mystery, too big a topic to discuss in this book. One perspective I find quite penetrating yet soothing in the face of unfathomable pain is that from the serenity prayer:

God, grant me the serenity
to accept the things I cannot change,
the courage to change the things I can,
and the wisdom to know the difference.
Living one day at a time,

enjoying one moment at a time;
accepting hardship as a pathway to
peace;
taking, as Jesus did,
this sinful world as it is,
not as I would have it;
trusting that You will make all things
right
if I surrender to Your will;
so that I may be reasonably happy in this
life
and supremely happy with You forever in
the next.
Amen. (Reinhold Niebuhr)

When there is no miracle in tough times, remain in God.

God won't waste any hurts.

Pray as much as possible. Remember his goodness. Surrender to his plans, trusting that when something bad happens, something good will come out of it.

CHAPTER 13

Moving Forward

Taste God's Goodness and Be Grateful

I am deeply grateful for all that's happened to me, good and bad. I still regret the mistakes I made in my first marriage that led to divorce and the imperfect parenting of my son. But I know and am thankful that Jesus's death and resurrection are sufficient to cover that.

God has wrapped me up with his amazing love and grace when I hit rock bottom and drifted to a dangerous zone. He has shown me his humor, patience, and sovereignty when I was silly, shallow, and demanding. He has trained me to let go and seek his kingdom first. I am still to be refined and polished in many ways. I still wish to hear his voice again if he allows. But at the top of my daily prayer list for myself is asking God to help me live a life that is worthy of his blessings.

I pray: "What can I do to thank you Lord for your salvation and blessings?"

It is this gratitude that propels me to devote myself to serving the church, God's people, at any price. Although my husband is a pastor, he never requires me to assist him with anything, nor imposes on me any duties or volunteer work at the church. I am prompted, though, from time to time by the Spirit to pray, visit, and help those in need whenever I can. And that gives me joy and contentment.

I have never thought of becoming a person like I am now, as less than a decade ago I was still driving full steam ahead in one of the world's top financial centers to attain financial security, personal recognition, and accomplishment. But here I am, living in Naples—one of the smallest towns in Texas, where poverty is widespread—to serve the church and the community alongside my pastor husband. It is no longer the accumulation of money and credentials that fascinates me. It is seeing people's transformation that makes my day. This will surely surprise a lot of people who knew me and worked with me during my thirties and forties. And I, myself, find this a big surprise, too.

Recall the Experiences to Practice Trust

Just like the Israelites in ancient times, I am not only forgetful and ungrateful, but I am fearful and untrusting even after having experienced God's miraculous rescue and healing time and again.

I gather that trust has to be practiced and learned. It is not just the remembering that needs to be intentional. It is the act of faith after the remembering that matters, and it needs to be practiced. Still, the remembering is like a precursor or fuel to the production of faith.

Just before Christmas 2019, I fell on a step of an escalator that leads up to a commercial building in Hong Kong. The spikes on the edge of the step were made of hard and sharp steel. It felt like I had been bitten by a wild animal. The immediate pain was piercing and throbbing. I sat on the floor after coming off from the escalator and saw blood dripping from my lower left leg onto my foot and shoe. I wanted to cry for help, but there wasn't anybody in sight. I prayed and asked God for help.

"God, please help me because I know you see this and you can."

I was so calm at that moment that I surprised even myself. I quickly looked into my handbag for a tissue to soak up the blood. I was trained in first aid, so I applied pressure to the visible wound to stop the bleeding. The bleeding stopped despite the very deep wound (which I found later would warrant a few stitches). I tended the wound myself for a few days, then went to the doctor for an X-ray to make sure there was no broken bone.

All these subsequent details are actually not important. The important fact for me is that there was no panic at the time I was hurt. I know where this peace and calm came from. It was from the experience and encounters with God in the past, knowing how he had faithfully healed and restored me or brought me through crises and uncertainty. I did not ask for a miracle; I knew I did not have to at that moment, because I was fully confident in the knowledge that God knew what was best for me.

What I needed most at that time was to rest assured in his peace, his care, and his divine plan.

Faith needs to be practiced, and my memories of all that has happened in the past adds fuel to the fire of faith. There was no miracle in the healing of the wound in December. The visible wound took almost one and a half months to heal, and there is still redness and knots underneath the new skin as I write this. There was no miracle, but there was certainty, peace, and gratitude in my heart for God's presence and closeness, and that was a sweet experience.

Chase after God, Not after Miracles

As discussed above, God does not intend to use miracles to draw us to him. We have seen numerous pieces of evidence that miracles do not necessarily lead to faith or submission to God.

God is the creator of the universe. He is the sovereign, almighty God, the one sustaining all lives and taking charge of all events on earth and in space. In him, nothing is impossible. He himself is the miracle.

God is holy; he cannot bear sins. Yet he loves us so much that he was willing to humble himself to become a human, take up all our sins, and die on the cross to pay for our debt. As one BSF leader has said, "God was so eager to form a relationship with us that he thought of a way to get rid of our sins without getting rid of us!"

God is not limited by time, power, or resources. Yet he loves us so much that in order to take up our sins as well as to reveal himself to us, he limited himself, sacrificed all his rights, and came to live thirty years of life going through all kinds of pain and suffering on earth. The birth, death, and resurrection of Jesus, God in flesh, revolutionized the whole of human history and brought hope to all creation.

God loves us so much that he is willing to bend down to listen to our prayers. As said by a preacher, we rarely have easy access or a direct telephone line to kings, national leaders, or royalty. But we can proceed to the throne of our almighty God anytime, anywhere. He is pleased when we pray to him and ask him for help and provision. He is always faithful and keeps his promises. He wants us to trust him and find joy in him. He has our best interest in mind.

Think about this again: the God who created the universe wants an intimate relationship with us and pursues us. He is the one who gives us the ultimate good. If there is any miracle, it is because of him and his love. He is the one who performed miracles throughout history.

So, what else can we hope for apart from God? If you have God, you already have the miracle. Let's hang onto his character, promises, and love. Don't chase after miracles; chase after God.

Chase after God and God alone.